Be Renewed

A Guide to the Sacrament of Reconciliation

Paul Turner

LITURGICAL PRESS

Collegeville, Minnesota

www.litpress.org

1   2   3   4   5   6   7   8   9

Library of Congress Cataloging-in-Publication Data

Names: Turner, Paul, author.
Title: Be renewed : a guide to the sacrament of reconciliation / Paul Turner.
Description: Collegeville, Minnesota : Liturgical Press, [2023] | Summary: "In this commentary on the revised English translation of The Order of Penance, Paul Turner explains in detail how the sacrament of renewal has itself undergone renewal since the first edition approved shortly after the Second Vatican Council. Turner highlights important elements within the revised translation and invites all Catholics to consider the sacrament anew"— Provided by publisher.
Identifiers: LCCN 2023009297 (print) | LCCN 2023009298 (ebook) | ISBN 9798400800146 (paperback) | ISBN 9798400800160 (epub) | ISBN 9798400800153 (pdf)
Subjects: LCSH: Penance. | Confession. | Sacraments.
Classification: LCC BX2260 .T78 2023 (print) | LCC BX2260 (ebook) | DDC 234/.166—dc23/eng/20230718
LC record available at https://lccn.loc.gov/2023009297
LC ebook record available at https://lccn.loc.gov/2023009298

"Be healed, be reconciled, be forgiven are the usual ways I have thought about the sacrament of penance, but Fr. Turner's title *Be Renewed* offers more than a one-time experience of this sacrament. His presentation of the extended history shows the efforts through the ages to make this an opportunity of spiritual and personal change, growth, and renewal. Beyond the central act of confession of sin and absolution, the various examples of penance services and examination of conscience open doorways to invite the kind of blessing, comfort, and personal peace offered by the communal prayer of the Church. This is an excellent resource for faith formation for all age groups in the Church."

—Sister Lois Paha, OP, DMin, Director of Formation
and Liturgy for the Diocese of Tucson

"Fr. Paul Turner's *Be Renewed* is an essential resource for all who work in pastoral ministry. Practical, informative, and engaging, this book provides the detailed and gentle guidance needed to celebrate the sacrament well. It demystifies terms, concepts, and structures and equips pastoral ministers to confidently provide for and promote reconciliation. *Be Renewed* will surely become a regular reference for confessors, catechists, directors of religious education, liturgists, and all who contribute to the faithful's understanding and experience of the Order of Penance."

—Matthew Reichert, Director of the Center for Learning,
Oregon Catholic Press

"Once again Father Paul Turner has expertly blended fine scholarship with keen pastoral skill. Thoroughly documented, *Be Renewed* offers parishioners and priests alike a comprehensive study of the new (2023) English translation of the Church's three rites of sacramental reconciliation and penance services. Fr. Turner provides a bonus resource by including his translation of the nine forms of an examination of conscience set in the context of a liturgical service—texts found in the draft of the revision but replaced by alternate texts in the published edition. *Be Renewed* offers much understanding, insight, and encouragement to those approaching the sacrament 'from either side of the screen.'"

—Rt. Rev. Kurt Stasiak, OSB, Archabbot of Saint Meinrad
    Archabbey

GREGORIO POLANO OSB

IN ADMIRATIONE EXEMPLORVM EIVS

CONVERSATIONIS MORVM

APERTÆ INDENTIDEM AD DEI VOCATIONES

AC REI REMISSIONIS

QVAM MVLTOS OBSTIPVIT

DEDICATVR HOC STVDIVM

ABBATI ET AVCTORIS AMICO

Contents

Acknowledgments

I wish to thank
    Ken Riley, who read
    Keith Stanfield, who wondered
    Olvin Giron, who clarified
    The penitents, who confessed
    My confessors, who forgave
    God, whose mercies are without number.

P.T.

Introduction

The sacrament of reconciliation draws many Catholics in increasing numbers and frequency. In the United States, members of the Hispanic community seem to seek out the sacrament more than their Anglo counterparts. A growing number of young adults finds spiritual support and comfort from this sacrament of healing. In spite of those examples, some other Catholics rarely, if ever, confess.

The Catholic Church revised its Order of Penance together along with many other rites shortly after the Second Vatican Council, optimistic that the treasures of this sacrament would serve generations to come in newer and more vibrant ways. The first English translation revealed new insights into the sacrament, especially in regard to the words of absolution and the possibility of communal celebrations.

A revised English translation invites Catholics to consider the sacrament anew. They may explore in greater depth its nature and the beauty of its effect. Due to the revision, some who have avoided this sacrament may rediscover the riches of periodic confession. Those who already use it frequently may hone their examination of conscience and their will to change their lives.

Renewal of life is difficult. Sometimes it requires more than frequent confession. Counselors, friends, and health-care teams can all assist personal growth. Still, this sacrament prepares a spiritual path upon which the faithful may walk in search of personal forgiveness, the repair of broken relationships, and a profound encounter with the mercy of God. They may enter the confessional nervous, but they will likely exit renewed.

Confessing Sins

Going to confession eases a conscience burdened by sin and aids one's return to God. Catholics probably sin as much as anyone else, so the Church provides a sacrament of encounter with the one who alone possesses the power to forgive: Jesus Christ, the Son of God. A priest, acting in the name of Christ, supplies this ministry.

Titles of the Sacrament

Frequently called "confession," the sacrament also goes by other titles: "reconciliation," for example, and "penance," as in the name of the official book for its celebration, The Order of Penance. These three names emphasize different aspects of the same sacrament.

"Confession" is the verbal declaration of one's sins. It presupposes the inner journey of one who has erred and admits wrongdoing in order to recommit to Christian values. Many parishes post times for this sacrament under the heading "Confessions," probably because the word connects most directly with the interior journey the penitent has walked and names the step that the penitent feels called to take.

"Penance" focuses on the discipline the penitent undertakes after confessing sin. During a confession, after relating one's sins, the penitent receives a penance from the priest. However, "penance" also holds a more generic meaning. It can refer to self-imposed discipline to atone for one's sins or to challenge oneself to lead a better life. During Lent, for example, many Catholics adopt penitential practices over its six weeks for this purpose.

"Reconciliation" is the richest of these terms because it signifies the ultimate goal of a confession—restoring a grace-filled relationship with God. This sacrament does not simply concern the action of the penitent, but the action of God, who forgives. This mutuality achieves for the penitent the reconciliation of a broken relationship. Additionally, the word suggests one's reconciliation with the Church. Sin disrupts a community; confessing it reconciles its members. As will be seen, those who revised The Order of Penance wanted to stress the overlooked ecclesial nature of reconciliation.

"Reconciling Penitents" first appeared as a heading in one of the earliest liturgical books, the eighth-century Gelasian Sacramentary. It signified a rite in which those who had been doing public penance for grave sin restored their normal relationship with the Church. This ancient description for the sacrament has returned in contemporary usage. The Order of Penance opens with three chapters describing the available formats for celebration; each of them calls its expression of the ritual "reconciling penitents."

The Titles in the Ritual Book

The Catholic Church publishes official books for its worship. This library provides services for well-known occasions such as the Mass, baptisms, weddings and funerals, as well as lesser-known occasions such as the blessing of an abbot, the dedication of an altar, and the consecration of religious men and women. For the sacrament of reconciliation, the liturgical book is called The Order of Penance. However, the early chapters more precisely describe ritual orders "for reconciling" penitents. The book includes optional texts such as an elaborate apparatus listing Scripture readings pertaining to the sacrament, as well as penitential rituals distinct from the sacrament. These services awaken a sense of repentance among the faithful and may lead them to celebrate the sacrament. Appendices include an examination of conscience. Therefore, the title of the book represents the breadth of its contents: three different ways of celebrating the sacrament, a variety of useful texts, a collection of prayer services suitable for different times of the liturgical year and for various subgroups of the faithful, all exploring the themes of penance, and appendices. The title of the book may seem to promote the word "penance" as the name for the sacrament, but the contents will call it more directly "reconciliation."

In 1963 the bishops participating in the Second Vatican Council authorized a renewal of the Church's worship in the Constitution on the Sacred Liturgy (*Sacrosanctum Concilium*). Much of the constitution pertains to the Mass, but in its section on sacraments it makes this declaration: "The rite and formulas of Penance are to be revised so that they more clearly express both the nature and effect of the sacrament" (72).[1]

In this single, laconic sentence, the constitution summarized several points: some dissatisfaction with the current rite, an acknowledgment that its words and actions inadequately expressed the meaning of the sacrament, and the charge to revise these for the good of the Church. To implement directives such as this one throughout the constitution, Pope St. Paul VI formed a Consilium of specialists to create and

---

1. Austin Flannery, ed., *Vatican Council II: Constitutions, Decrees, Declarations; The Basic Sixteen Documents* (Collegeville, MN: Liturgical Press, 2014), p. 141.

oversee the work of dozens of study groups that elaborated the specifics. In this case, the work was assigned to Study Group 23 bis (named "the second" because there was already a Study Group 23). The chair was Joseph Lécuyer, CSSp, professor of the Medieval Institute "John XXIII" at the Pontifical Lateran University. Members of the group included Franz Heggen, Franz Nikolasch, Zoltan Alszeghy, Paul Anciaux, Cassiano Floristán, Alfons Kirchgässner, Louis Ligier, Karl Rahner, Cyril Vogel, Pierre Jounel, Franco Sottocornola, Juan Antonio Gracía, Pelagio Visentin, Hans Bernhard Meyer, Kevin Donovan, and Gottardo Pasqualetti.[2]

The group favored restoring the medieval word "reconciliation" to better express the simultaneous action between God and the individual. Members cited another paragraph of the constitution, "Christ is always present in his Church, especially in liturgical celebrations" (7).[3] Pertinent Scripture passages explored the reconciliation of humanity with God:

> God . . . has reconciled us to himself through Christ and given us the ministry of reconciliation (2 Cor 5:18).
>
> [Christ] has now reconciled [you] in his fleshly body through his death (Col 1:22).
>
> We also boast of God through our Lord Jesus Christ, through whom we have now received reconciliation (Rom 5:11).
>
> [For it pleased the Father] through Christ to reconcile all things for him (Col 1:20).[4]

In this sacrament, then, Christ is present in his ministry of reconciling humanity with God.

---

2. Annibale Bugnini, *The Reform of the Liturgy, 1948–1975*, trans. Matthew J. O'Connell (Collegeville, MN: Liturgical Press, 1990), pp. 664, 671.

3. *Vatican Council II*, p. 120.

4. Sacra Congregatio Pro Cultu Divino, "Ordo Pænitentiæ," Schemata n. 386.2, De Pænitentia n. 13 (7 November 1972), p. 7.

To show one's reconciliation with the Church, the group cited several more passages from the Bible:

> If you bring your gift to the altar, and there recall that your brother has anything against you, leave your gift there at the altar, go first and be reconciled with your brother, and then come and offer your gift (Matt 5:23-24).
>
> [Christ] is our peace, he who made both one . . . that he might create in himself one new person instead of two, thus establishing peace, and might reconcile both with God in one body, through the cross, putting that enmity to death by it (Eph 2:14-16).
>
> And all this is from God, who has reconciled us to himself through Christ and given us the ministry of reconciliation, namely, God was reconciling the world to himself in Christ, not counting their trespasses against them and entrusting to us the message of reconciliation. So we are ambassadors for Christ, as if God were appealing through us. We implore you on behalf of Christ, be reconciled to God (2 Cor 5:18-20).[5]

Thus, the word "reconciliation" shows both divine and human action together. The study group believed that this communitarian dimension flowed naturally from the Council's themes.

Even the word "penance" prompted some discussion because of its spelling. Some liturgical books of the past and even the acts of the Second Vatican Council spelled the Latin word with an "o" instead of an "a": *pœnitentia* instead of *pænitentia*. The study group preferred the latter. The first is a source for the English word "pain," whereas the second is the source for "penance" and perhaps even relates to "penury." The true meaning of penance is not to subject someone to pain, but to

5. Schemata n. 386.2, p. 7.

invite a voluntary turning away from evil and toward good. Such a redirection may cause discomfort, but its primary goal is conversion of life. In common usage the word "penance" may imply something exterior, but in the spiritual sense it aims for the heart. Far from inflicting pain, the joy of conversion emanates from passages such as the parables of the lost sheep (Luke 15:7), the lost coin (Luke 15:10), and of the prodigal son (Luke 15:22-25). The study group noted that those parables celebrate reconciliation.[6]

Yet because the ritual book would contain more than the sacrament, it adopts separate terms. Each of the three forms of celebration is called an order for reconciling penitents, but the entire book is The Order of Penance.

A Moment in History

The Forms of Reconciliation

Evidence from the early centuries of Christianity indicates that believers always sought some way of restoring their pristine spiritual condition once perfected in baptism but since then soiled by sin. By the Middle Ages, the faithful who were repenting of sins that they committed after baptism entered an "order of penitents," to indicate their liminal state. This paralleled the order of catechumens, a group of those unbaptized who were seeking formation leading toward the rites of initiation. Usually on Ash Wednesday, each penitent approached the bishop, confessed their sins in private, and asked for penance. Then, in the presence of the gathered faithful, the bishop imposed hands on the sinner and assigned a penance. The penitent put on sackcloth and other penitential vestments, took a special place in the church for the Mass, and participated without receiving communion. The confession of one's

---

6. Consilium ad Exsequendam Constitutionem de Sacra Liturgia, Schemata n. 222, De Pænitentia 1 (31 March 1967), pp. 2–3.

sin and the execution of one's penance took place in public, not in secret, so these actions touched the whole community of the faithful.[7]

The reconciliation of these sinners usually took place on Holy Thursday. All gathered with the bishop for an elaborate ceremony of litanies, psalms, and antiphons, culminating in the bestowal of absolution from sin.[8] This enabled the penitents to return to communion during the Mass of the Lord's Supper. The ceremony, which had fallen into disuse, was removed from the Roman Pontifical published in 1962, just before the start of the Second Vatican Council.[9] However, its formulas, part of the Church's liturgical treasury, inspired some of the revisions to come.

A format for the confession of individual sins appeared in the Roman Ritual of 1614. The priest entered the designated place for confessions, vested in surplice and a violet stole. As each penitent approached, the priest admonished them to adopt humility of heart. The penitent kneeled and made the sign of the cross. The priest could request the penitent's state of life, the time since the last confession, and whether the penitent had fulfilled the imposed penance. The penitent confessed the sins previously discerned. The priest could instruct the penitent on the rudiments of the faith. The penitent made a general confession in the vernacular, such as the *Confiteor* ("I confess to almighty God"). Then the penitent spoke the specifics, helped if necessary by the priest to name the number, kind, and circumstances of the sins. The priest encouraged the penitent to lead a better life and offered a fitting penance.

---

7. Consilium ad Exsequendam Constitutionem de Sacra Liturgia, Schemata n. 272, De Pænitentia 5 (17 February 1968), pp. 9–10.

8. *Pontificale Romanum, Editio Princeps (1595–1596)*, ed. Manlio Sodi and Achille Maria Triacca (Vatican City: Libreria Editrice Vaticana, 1997), pp. 555–73.

9. *Pontificale Romanum*, ed. Anthony Ward, SM, and Cuthbert Johnson, OSB (Rome: CLV Edizioni Liturgiche, 1999).

Assuming that the gravity of the sin did not require a further time of penance, the priest gave absolution.[10]

Reform

The 1963 Constitution on the Sacred Liturgy sought to reform these rituals to express more clearly the nature and the effect of this sacrament. The revisers applied additional principles that the Second Vatican Council had advocated.[11] For example, the Dogmatic Constitution on the Church, *Lumen Gentium*, declared that Christ "established and constantly sustains here on earth his holy church, the community of faith, hope and charity, as a visible structure through which he communicates truth and grace to everyone" (8).[12] Furthermore, "Those who approach the sacrament of Penance obtain pardon through God's mercy for the offense committed against him, and are, at the same time, reconciled with the church which they have wounded by their sins and which by charity, by example and by prayer labors for their conversion" (11).[13] The revisers therefore wanted to express the ecclesial dimension of the sacrament of penance—how sin affects the community, and how the community prays for the sinner.

In a decree dedicated to the pastoral office of bishops, *Christus Dominus*, the Council declared that pastors "must bear constantly in mind how much the sacrament of penance contributes to the development of the christian life and should therefore be readily available for the hearing of the confessions of the faithful. If necessary, they should call on other priests

10. *Rituale Romanum, Editio prima post typicam anno 1953 promulgata*, Titulus IV, Caput I and Caput II (Rome: CLV Edizioni Liturgiche, 2001), pp. 129–35.

11. Schemata n. 222, p. 1. See also Pierre-Marie Gy, "Penance and Reconciliation," in *The Church at Prayer: An Introduction to the Liturgy*, ed. Aimé Georges Martimort, vol. 3, *The Sacraments*, trans. Matthew J. O'Connell (Collegeville, MN: Liturgical Press, 1988), p. 114.

12. *Vatican Council II*, p. 9.

13. *Vatican Council II*, p. 15.

who are fluent in different languages to help in this work" (30 §2).[14] The purpose of the sacrament is not just the forgiveness of one's sins, but the development of the Christian life. Pastors need to do their part.

The Council also issued a decree on the Ministry and Life of Priests, *Presbyterorum Ordinis*. In listing the duties of priests, the decree states, "by the sacrament of Penance [priests] reconcile sinners with God and the church," and that "in the spirit of Christ the pastor, they instruct [the faithful] to submit their sins to the church with a contrite heart in the sacrament of Penance" (5).[15] The Council laid out the principle that this sacrament achieves reconciliation not only with God, but also with the Church.

The revisers summarized four points from these excerpts: sin is both an offense against God and a wound on the Church; the sinner's reconciliation is both with God and with the Church; the entire Church works together for the conversion of sinners through charity, example, and prayers; and the sacrament of penance has value for nurturing the Christian life.[16] The group felt that the current order of penance sufficiently expressed only the last of these points. In the revision, they strove to include the other three.

The revisers relied upon other principles of the reform from the Constitution on the Sacred Liturgy: "the rites should radiate a noble simplicity" (34);[17] "in liturgical celebrations, a more ample, more varied, and more suitable selection of readings from sacred scripture should be restored" (35 §1),[18] and "rites which are meant to be celebrated in common, with the faithful present and actively participating, should as far as possible be celebrated in that way rather than by an individual

14. *Vatican Council II*, p. 304.
15. *Vatican Council II*, pp. 324–25.
16. Schemata n. 222, p. 2.
17. *Vatican II*, p. 129.
18. *Vatican II*, p. 130.

and quasi-privately" (27).[19] All these principles would express another reminder from the Council, that sacraments "not only presuppose faith, but by words and objects they also nourish, strengthen, and express it" (59).[20] The revisers desired to respond faithfully to the request, "In order that sound tradition be retained, and yet the way remain open to legitimate progress, a careful investigation—theological, historical, and pastoral—should always, first of all, be made into each section of the liturgy which is to be revised" (23).[21] They used these directives from the Council as templates for their work.[22]

Study Group 23 bis produced several drafts. Its members received feedback from the Vatican's Congregation for Divine Worship. They consulted 614 sixteen-year-old students in fifteen schools from different regions in England (Birkdale, Sheffield, Oxford, Kirby, Northampton, and Hartlepool), and received comments from Catholics in other countries such as France, Scotland, the United States, Australia, and Africa.[23] The study group strove for greater vitality in celebrating the sacrament, inspiring penitents and priests to adopt a less mechanistic approach and to stress the communal sense of the celebration.[24]

Devotional confessions were common at the time of the Council—occasions when the penitent may have confessed past sins already forgiven or behaviors not completely sinful. The revisers realized that the practice provided some spiritual comfort, but they anxiously warned that the faithful not confuse a devotional confession with the sacrament.[25]

The new rite required time to develop. The revised Order of Mass took priority and was finalized in 1969. Work on The

---

19. *Vatican II*, p. 128.
20. *Vatican II*, p. 138.
21. *Vatican II*, p. 127.
22. Schemata n. 222, p. 2, and Schemata n. 272, p. 5.
23. Schemata n. 272, p. 2, and Bugnini, p. 664.
24. Bugnini, p. 665.
25. Schemata 272, p. 2.

Order of Penance came to a close several years later in 1974.[26] The English translation was published in 1975.[27]

The revised rite asked the priest to welcome each penitent and encourage them to trust in God's mercy. It added an optional reading from Sacred Scripture, and it concluded with praise of God's mercy and a formal dismissal. Many of the new texts came from Scripture, and the whole liturgy was adaptable for a large number of penitents. The reforms stressed that God's mercy serves as the source of grace, that reconciliation has its place within the paschal mystery, that the Holy Spirit has a role in forgiveness, and that the community is involved because of the shared impact of one's sin and the responsibility of the Church to help the sinner.[28]

The 1975 English translation ultimately yielded to a revision in 2023. The work resulted from the updated principles of translation provided by the Congregation for Divine Worship and the Discipline of the Sacraments in its 2001 instruction *Liturgiam Authenticam*, and by Pope Francis in his 2017 Apostolic Letter *Magnum Principium*, which assigned more translation authority to conferences of bishops. The changes in 2023 applied only to the English translation and clarified a few points within the ritual. Nonetheless, any revised book naturally draws attention back to the work that the revisers completed in 1974.

Many Catholics celebrate the sacrament of penance unaware of these revisions and their implications. The revised English translation of the Rite of Penance, now called The Order of Penance (OP), invites Catholics to rediscover the themes that the Council sought to illuminate by rethinking the celebration of the sacrament of reconciliation.

---

26. *Ordo Pænitentiæ*, Editio Typica (Vatican City: Typis Polyglottis Vaticanis, 1974).

27. *The Rite of Penance* (New York: Catholic Book Publishing Co., 1975).

28. Bugnini, p. 680.

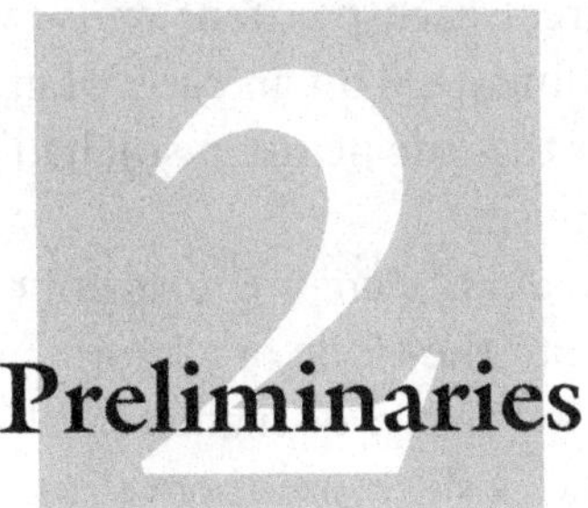

Preliminaries

Places for Confession

Penitents usually confess their sins to a priest at a designated place inside a church (OP 12). Some churches have a single confessional; others have many.

Confessionals arrived fairly late in Church history—as did the practice of confessing privately to a priest. The early Church provided means of forgiveness, but a penitent's consultation with a priest did not evolve until the eighth century when monks in Ireland popularized the practice in their own country and in the missions where they served.[1] The 1565 Council of Milan under Cardinal St. Charles Borromeo introduced the requirement for a fixed grille between the priest and the penitent, especially to establish propriety when hearing the confessions of women.[2] Confessionals were to be in a public area of the church for the same reason. Pope Paul V included the provision for a grille in the Roman Ritual of 1614.[3]

1. Schemata n. 272, pp. 12–15.
2. Schemata n. 222, p. 3.
3. *Rituale Romanum*, Titulus IV, Caput I:8, p. 130.

Nonetheless, early drafts for the revised ritual removed the requirement and envisioned an open setting where the priest would kindly greet each penitent and invite them to sit or kneel.[4] In a commentary on an early draft, Balthasar Fischer wanted it clearer that the penitent still had the option of confessing anonymously.[5]

The revised Order of Penance does not require a fixed grille for confessions, but the Code of Canon Law asks that confessionals so equipped always be made available in an open space for penitents who wish to use them (964 §2). Commenting on this in 1998, the Pontifical Council for Legislative Texts also gave the priest the option to hear confessions anonymously, even if the penitent preferred to see him face-to-face.[6] The USCCB's complementary norms on confessionals say that churches are to have a sufficient number of places for confessions, and that these should be visible, accessible, and furnished with a fixed grille. Provision should also be made for those who wish to confess face-to-face, though respecting the right of priests to hear confessions behind a grille.[7]

As the ritual evolved after the Council, many parishes converted their confessionals into reconciliation rooms where a penitent enjoyed the choice of confessing anonymously or

4. Coetus XXIII bis, Schemata n. 251, De Pænitentia, 2 (15 October 1967), allegatum II:1; and Consilium ad Exsequendam Constitutionem de Sacra Liturgia, Schemata n. 265, De Pænitentia 3 [between 7 and 25 December 1967], p. 2.

5. Coetus XXIII bis, Consilium ad Exsequendam Constitutionem de Sacra Liturgia, Schemata n. 267 (25 January 1968), p. 1.

6. *Interpretationes Authenticæ*, https://www.vatican.va/roman_curia /pontifical_councils/intrptxt/documents/rc_pc_intrptxt_doc_22091998 _authentic-interp_lt.html.

7. United States Conference of Catholic Bishops, Canonical Affairs & Church Governance, Complementary Norms, canon 964 §2, https://www .vatican.va/roman_curia/pontifical_councils/pccs/documents/rc_pc_pccs _doc_20020228_church-internet_en.html.

face-to-face. Many penitents find the second option more conducive to making progress in the spiritual life, conversing with the priest openly to receive his guidance, utilizing visual tools such as facial expressions and body language. Others, however, prefer anonymity, perhaps to minimize their embarrassment over their sins and to focus more directly on the disembodied words of the priest.

Confessionals of the past addressed the safety concerns of women, but those concerns, formerly expressed in the 1917 code of law (909–910) were not included in the 1983 code (964). Since then, new concerns have arisen about the protection of children. Consequently, some advocates call for a safeguard glass pane in or adjacent to the confessional door so that anyone outside may view the penitent inside. Some confessionals are not enclosed rooms, but open fixtures occupying a space against an interior church wall; the priest sits in a curtained area, and the penitent kneels next to him, in full view of others in the church.

Posture is left entirely to the penitent. In the ritual before the conciliar reforms, the penitent knelt. In the drafts of the reformed rite, the priest offered the penitent the option to kneel or sit.[8] In the end, the ritual does not indicate the penitent's posture. In practice, a confessional usually provides a kneeler for an anonymous confession. Many reconciliation rooms feature a chair for the penitent. At some communal penitential services, penitents stand while they confess to a priest, who also stands.

In the digital age, many people wonder if confessions could not be celebrated through electronic media instead of a designated physical space where priest and penitent meet in person. Even before the internet, the same question came up in reference to telephone calls, which not only lacked the sharing of common space but failed to ensure the protection of the seal

---

8. For example, Schemata n. 265, p. 2.

of confession. Someone could eavesdrop on a conversation that must be held secret and sacred.

Still, many Catholics watch a celebration of the Mass on screens at home because they find it spiritually enriching. Even the Vatican has declared that blessings and indulgences can be granted to those who participate digitally at certain events, such as the pope's *Urbi et Orbi* blessings and the virtual rituals of a pandemic.[9] Some believe that confessions could occupy a similar arena.

However, reconciliation is neither a blessing nor an indulgence. It is a sacrament like baptism, confirmation, the Eucharist, and anointing of the sick. It requires physical presence for its celebration. Even in marriage, if one party cannot be present for the ceremony, a physical proxy stands in. Sacraments are celebrations of the complete person. They need more than visual and aural transmission. The Vatican summed up its position in this way:

> Virtual reality is no substitute for the Real Presence of Christ in the Eucharist, the sacramental reality of the other sacraments, and shared worship in a flesh-and-blood human community. There are no sacraments on the Internet; and even the religious experiences possible there by the grace of God are insufficient apart from real-world interaction with other persons of faith.[10]

Penitents may choose the place for their confession. Some avail themselves of their parish church. Others, to ensure

9. Decree of the Apostolic Penitentiary on the granting of special Indulgences to the faithful in the current pandemic, 20 March 2020, https://press.vatican.va/content/salastampa/en/bollettino/pubblico/2020/03/20/200320c.html.

10. Pontifical Council for Social Communications, "The Church and Internet," 22 February 2002, n. 9, https://www.vatican.va/roman_curia/pontifical_councils/pccs/documents/rc_pc_pccs_doc_20020228_church-internet_en.html.

greater anonymity, may choose a priest at a different place. The choice belongs to the penitent.

Vesting for Confession

Vesture is left to the priest. Before the reforms, the ritual instructed him to wear a cassock, surplice, and violet stole. The drafts offered some options. One allowed the priest to wear an alb instead of cassock and surplice.[11] Another noted that it was difficult to find even a stole when hearing confessions at the unexpected request of a Catholic on board a train or while on a camping trip.[12] In those cases, the priest administered the sacrament without putting on vestments.

One draft noted a discussion on the color: Many in France preferred green, the sign of hope, especially since the traditional color, violet, was now being permitted instead of the color black for offices and Masses of the dead.[13] It was also noted that some priests heard confessions wearing only a stole over their normal clothes, and that violet remained a sign of penance and of interior conversion.[14] A late draft called for the priest to wear a stole where it was the custom, but did not designate any color.[15] Another said, "The use of the stole depends on the times and circumstances of the place, and is left to the judgment of pastors."[16]

Although The Order of Penance does not specify how the priest vests, the penitent deserves visual reassurance that the person hearing confessions is indeed a priest. The minister would appropriately wear at least a stole over clerical dress, or over an

11. Schemata n. 251 allegatum II, p. 1.
12. Schemata n. 222, p. 4.
13. Schemata n. 251 allegatum II, p. 1.
14. Schemata n. 251 allegatum II, p. 8.
15. Schemata n. 272, p. 50.
16. Coetus XXIII bis, Consilium ad Exsequendam Constitutionem de Sacra Liturgia, Schemata n. 318 (7 October 1968), p. 2.

alb or cassock and surplice. In unexpected circumstances the priest may hear a confession without any specific vesture.

Occasions for Confession

Parishes generally post regular times when priests are available to celebrate reconciliation. Penitents who find the schedule inconvenient may make an appointment for a different time agreeable to the priest. Some penitents spontaneously request a confession upon seeing a priest doing something else.

The Order of Penance says that confessions may be heard at any time on any day, but the faithful should strive to approach the sacrament at the scheduled times (13). Penitents can help their priests by taking advantage of the schedule that they have made. Priests have many responsibilities, and other people have already requested some of their time each day. Penitents can help priests fulfill their duties by observing the parish schedule or arranging a time in advance.

Often a priest hears confessions just before Mass. When he is also the celebrant of the Mass, he may occasionally have to stop confessions in order to prepare himself for the Eucharist. This disappoints priest and penitent, but it is completely unpredictable. No one knows how many penitents may show up for confessions.

Priests in general would love to oblige the spontaneous request for confession, but they are not always able to help. If a priest is greeting worshipers at the door of the church before Mass begins, he is spending his time to connect with the people with whom he usually has only a few moments each week. If someone requests an unscheduled confession before Mass, the request takes the priest away from another pastoral duty that will have an impact on other parishioners who reasonably expect to see him at their appointed time.

Priests are discouraged from hearing confessions during Mass. The 1967 Instruction on Eucharistic Worship, *Eucha-*

risticum Mysterium, from the Sacred Congregation of Rites, noted that two liturgical celebrations are not to take place in church at the same time because it would distract the faithful's attention (17). Those going to confession would have to withdraw from participating fully, consciously, and actively at the Mass while celebrating another sacrament. If they were to return to the Mass, they would not have given their full attention to the complete order of worship, creating a new spiritual malaise while healing another. The same instruction explicitly asks the faithful to go to confession outside of Mass so that the sacrament of penance can be celebrated calmly and with great fruit, without interfering with those who have gathered for the purpose of celebrating the Eucharist (35).[17]

In 2001, however, the Congregation for Divine Worship and the Discipline of the Sacraments did permit priests who were not celebrating or concelebrating Mass to hear the confessions of the faithful during a Mass if this provided aid to the penitents.[18] Pope St. John Paul II repeated this permission in his Apostolic Letter in the form of *motu proprio, Misericordia Dei* (2). The same Congregation's 2004 instruction *Redemptionis Sacramentum* cited both these sources (76) and repeated the provision that the sacrament of penance may not be united to the Mass in a single liturgical celebration. For the integrity of the two liturgies, Mass and reconciliation, those participating fully in a confession do not presume also to participate incompletely in a simultaneous Mass.

Lent is a most appropriate time of year for the sacrament, as The Order of Penance notes (13). An older liturgical tradition kept Good Friday and Holy Saturday completely free from the celebration of sacraments, but the Congregation for Divine Worship and the Discipline of the Sacraments declared in 1977 that it interpreted the rubric in the Roman Missal at the

17. https://adoremus.org/1967/05/eucharisticum-mysterium/.
18. *Notitiae* 419–20, vol. 37, 6–7:259–60.

beginning of Good Friday to mean only that the Mass could not be celebrated on those two days.[19] The Congregation for Divine Worship then permitted the celebration of penance and the anointing of the sick on Good Friday and Holy Saturday in its 1988 Circular Letter Concerning Preparation and Celebration of Easter Feasts (61 and 75).[20] The third edition of the Roman Missal excludes the celebration of all the sacraments on the same two days—except for penance and the anointing of the sick.[21]

Canon 914 states that children make their first confession before first communion. Those preparing for their first communion in the Catholic Church are to celebrate the sacrament of reconciliation beforehand. This applies not only to children, but also to adults previously baptized in other Christian denominations, who are to be received into the full communion of the Catholic Church. Unbaptized adults and children of catechetical age do not confess their sins before their first communion. They celebrate the three sacraments of initiation in the same ceremony, usually the Easter Vigil, and thus receive their first communion after all their sins have been forgiven through the waters of baptism. They alone make their first confession after their first communion.

Canon 989 requires the faithful to confess all grave sins at least once a year. This applies to all those who have reached the age of discretion, which precedes first communion. This coheres with canon 920 §1, which requires each of the faithful to receive communion once a year, and canon 920 §2, which requires the fulfillment of this precept during Easter Time. Devout Catholics will want to receive communion much more frequently than once a year. Easter makes the most appropriate

---

19. *Notitiae, "Ad Missale Romanum,"* 137, 12:602.

20. https://www.ewtn.com/catholicism/library/circular-letter-concerning-preparation-and-celebration-of-easter-feasts-2168.

21. Roman Missal, Friday of the Passion of the Lord [Good Friday], 1.

time of year to fulfill the duty because Jesus left his Body and Blood under sacramental signs, and those who participate in holy communion are sharing in the Body and Blood of the risen Christ. Easter is the time when adults and children of catechetical age receive their mystagogical formation in the sacraments they received at the Vigil. It is the time of great eucharistic celebration. Before receiving communion on any day, those conscious of grave sin are to celebrate the sacrament of reconciliation. The combination of these canons, commonly called one's "Easter Duty," requires confession of grave sins at least once a year so that the person becomes eligible to receive communion within the same interval.

Preparing to Confess

Before confessing sins, the penitent undergoes an examination of conscience to determine the areas that beg for reconciliation. A variety of catechetical aids exists in print and online. The Order of Penance itself offers an example (Appendix III). Other models appeared in one of the last drafts.[22] One of these used lines from the letters of St. Paul as springboards for reflection: Galatians 6:2 about carrying one another's burdens, 2 Corinthians 9:6-7 about sharing one's possessions happily, 1 Corinthians 1:10 about abandoning divisions and having one mind, and 2 Corinthians 11:28-29 about caring for all in the Church.[23]

The published edition uses a similar idea, but changed these points of reflection from the epistles of Paul to statements of Jesus from the gospels: Matthew 22:37 about loving God with all one's heart, John 15:12 about loving one another as

22. Sacra Congregatio pro Cultu Divino, Schemata n. 387 addendum I, De Pænitentia 14 (30 November 1972), pp. 33–47. See chapter 7 of this book for translations of these.

23. Schemata n. 387 addendum I, pp. 37–38.

Jesus loved, and John 14:21 about loving Christ by keeping his commandments (OP Appendix III:3).

The Order of Penance prefaces these with some concerns that the Roman Ritual wanted the priest to investigate during the confession: one should come to confession with a sincere desire for conversion, prepare to confess grave sins omitted in the past, and carry out the penance from the previous confession with the purpose of amending one's life (OP Appendix III:2).

As an alternative formula for an examination of conscience, many people benefit from a review of the Old Testament's Ten Commandments or the New Testament's Beatitudes. Many look back over their thoughts and actions at the end of each day to prepare a good summary of their spiritual life. Many pay attention to the concerns that arise from a troubled conscience.

Whatever tool one uses, the time before a confession helps each penitent encounter their true self with honesty. The examination of conscience helps them put their moral failure into words and gives them courage to confess their sin to a priest.

Preparing to Reconcile

The priest, too, prepares for hearing the confession and offering absolution. He is to call upon the Holy Spirit for the gifts of light and charity (OP 15). This simple instruction reminds the priest that he does not enter the confessional alone, but as an ambassador of God. He relies upon the Holy Spirit to offer good counsel, to reconcile the sinner, and to carry himself throughout as a model of Christian charity.

The Order for Reconciling Individual Penitents

The first chapter of The Order of Penance contains the procedure for individual reconciliation. It concerns the form of confession that most people know best: a penitent encounters a priest one-on-one. The priest hears the confession, offers absolution, and guides the penitent toward reconciliation with God and the Church.

Before the reform, the Roman Ritual described this order of service in narrative form, relating what the penitent and priest do, rather than in scripted form, telling what the penitent and priest say.[1] The 1974 revision lays out a confession in a more recognizably liturgical format with instructions for actions and spoken words (OP 41–47). Every confession still has an improvisatory feel, but it follows a liturgical outline from greeting to dismissal.

The Reception of the Penitent

The liturgy begins when the penitent comes to confess (OP 41). This seems obvious, but this first rubric echoes a change

---

1. *Rituale Romanum*, Titulus IV, Caput I:6–26, pp. 130–34.

to the first rubric in the Order of Mass. In the past, the Missal said that Mass began after the priest was vested. With the reforms, the Missal now says that Mass begins when the people have gathered (Order of Mass 1). The change acknowledged that what ensues should not be construed as the priest's Mass, but rather the celebration of the Eucharist by the entire People of God. Their presence precedes the beginning of the eucharistic liturgy. Similarly, The Order of Penance says that its liturgy begins when the penitent comes. The sudden presence of the Church, represented by the penitent and the priest, sets in motion the celebration of the sacrament of reconciliation.

The reception of the penitent has three components: The priest informally greets the penitent. The penitent initiates the sign of the cross. The priest invites the penitent to have trust in God. Then an optional fourth element may precede the confession of sins: a reading from Sacred Scripture (OP 41–43).

In practice, many Catholics begin their confession a different way. They start not by receiving the priest's welcome, nor making the sign of the cross, nor listening for the priest's invitation to trust, nor a Scripture reading, but with the formula, "Bless me, Father, for I have sinned." Some penitents say this and begin enumerating their sins even before the priest can open his mouth in welcome. The revised reception of the penitent has been in place since 1974, but few priests and penitents seem to have implemented it. The revisers of this liturgy reformulated the opening of a confession to express the nature and effect of the sacrament, as the Constitution on the Sacred Liturgy had requested.

The previous rite described a different opening: The penitent, having been encouraged to adopt appropriate humility in mind and demeanor, knelt down and made the sign of the cross.[2] The priest inquired about the penitent's state of life, duration since the last confession, completion of the penance,

---

2. *Rituale Romanum*, Titulus IV, Caput I:11, p. 131.

whether past confessions were thorough, and whether the penitent had conducted an examination of conscience.[3]

At their first meeting, the revisers questioned these instructions. They wanted explicit permission for the penitent to sit because episcopal conferences could determine the establishment of reconciliation rooms that made such posture possible. They thought that the confessor could fittingly begin with some words of greeting, especially if both persons were seated in the same room. They found the priest's questions from the Roman Ritual unnecessary, preferring him to create instead an atmosphere of trust that the penitent had come prepared.[4] This changed in the final drafts, which asked each penitent unknown to the priest to reveal their circumstances to him.[5] The revisers avoided creating a fixed formula, preferring to keep the greeting free and spontaneous from person to person.[6]

In the revised ritual, as noted above, many of the concerns from the priest's inquiry of the former rite have moved into the third appendix. Before coming to the confessional, penitents are to review their previous confession—whether any sins had been omitted and if the penance had been completed—and then examine their conscience. The revision presumes that the penitent already comes with the proper demeanor and has prepared to confess past faults in humility. Ordinarily, the priest need not inquire about these points.

The Priest's Greeting

Once the penitent has entered, the priest speaks first. Resembling a host, he takes this polite initiative. He informally welcomes the penitent with kindness and offers a greeting with friendly words (OP 41). He may fulfill this simply by saying,

---

3. *Rituale Romanum*, Titulus IV, Caput I:12, p. 131.
4. Schemata n. 222, p. 5.
5. Schemata n. 386, p. 21; and Schemata n. 387, p. 26.
6. Schemata n. 251 allegatum II, p. 8.

"Good afternoon," or "Welcome." Or he may craft his own warm greeting, already suggesting the mercy that the penitent has come in hope to receive. The drafts permitted a customary Christian greeting from various parts of the world: "Praised be Jesus Christ" or "Peace and good," for example.[7] In Spanish, the priest may begin with words of prayer to the most pure Virgin Mary, "*Ave Maria purísima,*" expecting the sinful penitent to respond with an affirmation of Mary's sinlessness, "*Sin pecado concebida.*" The liturgy avoids a formula here to make the reception of the penitent sincere, spontaneous, and appropriate to each person.

A similar instruction appears at the beginning of a wedding and in the admission of an unbaptized person into the first stage of the catechumenate. At a wedding, in the opening moments, the presider draws near to the couple to reassure them that the Church shares their joy and invites them to make the transition from the day's secular concerns outside the church into a true spiritual celebration inside the church (Order of Celebrating Matrimony 46 and 49, for example). Those aspiring to become catechumens may naturally feel nervous about the first public declaration of their budding faith, so the presider strives to ease the tension by sharing the joyful welcome of the community that the inquirers wish to join (Rite of Christian Initiation of Adults 49, for example).

In all these instances, the rubric basically tells the presider to be kind. It requires something more than reading words and performing the actions in the liturgical book. The presider's humane demeanor conveys the deep sense of the most interpersonal liturgies of the Roman Rite. In the case of reconciliation, he has already prepared for this encounter when he called upon the Holy Spirit for light and charity (OP 15). Now, in the joy of the Spirit, he greets the penitent with friendly words.

7. Schemata n. 272, p. 22.

Many of the drafts also had the priest issue a courteous invitation to kneel or sit.[8] This eventually seemed unnecessary because the presence of furniture would make the choice clear. The revisers acknowledged an overall concern that some penitents experienced great difficulty and even repulsion when approaching a confessor.[9] Confession is hard enough without the priest's unpleasant attitude making it more difficult. His words of greeting now intend to ease the first contact.

The Sign of the Cross

The penitent makes the sign of the cross while speaking the words associated with it, and the priest may join if this seems appropriate (OP 42). This is more easily accomplished if the two are facing each other, visibly sharing the action, but it works even when a grille separates them.

When the former ritual instructed penitents to kneel and make the sign of the cross, it did not specify whether they spoke the words aloud while making the gesture.[10] When the revisers set to work, the first several drafts omitted the sign of the cross altogether.[11] It only reappeared in the last drafts, where the priest and the penitent were to sign themselves with

---

8. Schemata n. 265, p. 2; Schemata n. 279, p. 50; Schemata n. 279 bis, p. 5; Schemata n. 297, p. 7; Schemata n. 312, p. 5; Schemata n. 318, p. 5; Schemata n. 361, p. 47; and Schemata n. 386, p. 21.

9. Schemata n. 272, p. 22.

10. *Rituale Romanum*, Titulus IV, Caput I:11, p. 131.

11. Schemata n. 265, p. 2; Coetus XXIII bis, Consilium ad Exsequendam Constitutionem de Sacra Liturgia, Schemata n. 279, De Pænitentia 6 (16 March 1968), p. 50; Coetus XXIII bis, Consilium ad Exsequendam Constitutionem de Sacra Liturgia, Schemata n. 279 bis, De Pænitentia 6a (22 April 1968), p. 5; Consilium ad Exsequendam Constitutionem de Sacra Liturgia, Schemata n. 297, De Pænitentia 7 (2 July 1968), p. 7; Coetus XXIII bis, Consilium ad Exsequendam Constitutionem de Sacra Liturgia, Schemata n. 312, De Pænitentia 8 (28 September 1968), p. 5; Schemata n. 318, p. 5; and Sacra Congregatio pro Cultu Divino, Schemata n. 361, De Pænitentia 12 (31 January 1970), p. 47.

the cross, while together declaring aloud the traditional words in the name of the Trinity.[12]

The revised Order of Penance assigns the duty to the penitent and allows the priest to join (OP 42). Seeing the actual words of the sign of the cross near the beginning of this ritual may not attract much attention, but this is the first explicit instruction in history to begin a confession with both the words and the gesture of the sign of the cross. In contrast to the Mass, where the priest speaks these words, and the people join him only in the gesture and the final Amen, in the sacrament of reconciliation the penitent speaks the words like a presider, advancing the liturgy forward.

The draft that introduced the words offered an interpretation: when the priest and penitent together sign themselves with the cross, they proclaim the reconciliation of sinners once sealed in the passion of Christ.[13] This sign and its words show the revisers' intent to bring to the fore the paschal mystery, one of the great themes of the Second Vatican Council.

Invitation to Trust

The priest invites the penitent to trust in God. The priest may use his own words, but The Order of Penance offers him several formulas (OP 42, 67–71). Some of these are drawn from Scripture passages: Ezekiel 33:11; Luke 5:32; and 1 John 2:1-2. Others are non-biblical words of encouragement.

At the first meeting, the revisers envisioned something more. They recommended, as far as possible, that the penitent and priest begin with some words of prayer: a brief psalm, the Lord's Prayer, or a few verses from a gospel, followed by a time of silence.[14]

12. Schemata n. 386, p. 21; and Schemata n. 387, p. 26.
13. Schemata n. 386, p. 11.
14. Schemata n. 222, p. 5.

Later the group recommended specific psalms: 6, 32, 38, 51, 102, 130, 143, or even Isaiah 12:1-6 or some other prayer.[15] This proposed prayer in common was to express the role of the community in reconciliation.[16] The reading and common prayer endured through many of the drafts.[17] However, the published edition kept here only some words of encouragement—from within or outside of Scripture. It created an optional separate space for a reading from Scripture.

In the invitation to trust, the priest invokes the God of light to give the penitent living knowledge and even a certain hope in the mercy of the Father. The revisers thus connected the sign of the cross with this prayer of the priest. The awareness of sin would lead to despair if not for the cross of Christ by which God reconciled the world in mercy.[18] The same late draft gave two examples for what the priest could say: "The Lord does not desire the death of the sinner, but rather that he be converted and live. Trust in him" (see Ezek 33:11); or "The Lord Jesus did not come to call the just but sinners. Trust in him" (see Matt 9:13; Mark 2:17; or Luke 5:32).[19] Versions of these remain in OP 67 and 68.

A late draft replaced the suggested psalms with a longer list of individual verses, including 1 John 1:9; 1 John 2:1-2; Hebrews 4:16; 2 Maccabees 1:4-5; and Psalm 67:2. It also added the two non-biblical encouragements that now appear in The Order of Penance 69 and 70, and a third one that resembles the one in OP 42.[20]

15. Schemata n. 251 allegatum II, p. 2.

16. Schemata n. 265, p. 4.

17. Schemata n. 265, p. 2; Schemata n. 279, p. 50; Schemata n. 279 bis, p. 5; Schemata n. 297, p. 7; Schemata n. 312, p. 5; Schemata n. 318, p. 5; and Schemata n. 361, p. 47.

18. Schemata n. 386, p. 12.

19. Schemata n. 386, p. 21. See also Schemata n. 387, p. 26.

20. Schemata n. 387, p. 41.

That non-biblical encouragement had gone through many revisions. At the first meeting, the revisers recommended that the confessor bless the penitent with a formula, such as, "May the Lord be in your heart and on your lips that you may confess all your sins worthily and well." Those words appeared in the 1597 Ritual of Constance, and Charles Borromeo recommended using them.[21] They clearly derive from the blessing that the priest gives the deacon before the deacon proclaims the gospel at Mass (Order of Mass 14).

The revisers later changed the words to fit more contemporary concerns: "May the Lord be in your heart and on your lips that you may confess your sins in a contrite spirit."[22] It was further simplified: "May the Lord be in your heart that you may confess your sins in a contrite spirit," or "May the Lord shine his light on you and open your heart that you may confess your sins confident of his mercy." The penitent responded, "Amen."[23]

A later draft changed it again to the one that now appears in OP 42.[24] The next draft gave the two non-biblical options that now appear as OP 69 and 70.[25] The group continually stressed the optional nature of this introductory blessing.

On May 8, 1969, the Consilium of Pope Paul VI ceased to work independently and became part of the Congregation for Divine Worship, which continued the work on this revision. The Congregation continued its consultation by circulating these proposals for the renewal of confession. The new opening of the ritual had its critics. In negative comments about the entire draft, Cardinal Karol Wojtyła, the future Pope John Paul II, thought the ceremony would take too long, especially

21. Schemata n. 222, p. 5.
22. Schemata n. 272, p. 50.
23. Schemata n. 279 bis, p. 1.
24. Schemata n. 386, p. 21.
25. Schemata n. 387, p. 41.

given the lines of penitents during Lent and Advent in Poland. He also thought that the revision overstressed familiarity, dialogue, and direction, rather than the nature of repentance, identified by a humble confession of individual sins.[26]

In the end, the reception of the penitent is meant to flow freely. The priest welcomes each one with kindness. The penitent initiates the sign of the cross. The priest encourages the penitent to trust in God's mercy.

The Reading of the Word of God (Optional)

The priest may read a passage from the Bible or recite one from memory. He thus announces the mercy of God and the call of humanity to conversion (OP 43). Over a dozen options appear in OP 72–84, all but two from the New Testament. To introduce several of these, the priest explicitly invites the penitent to listen. The priest may choose from the more extensive list of citations in the reconciliation of several penitents (OP 101–201). Or the priest and penitent may use some other reading (OP 84). That instruction suggests that penitents may read a passage that they found helpful in preparing their confession. Although this option has been in place since 1974, not many penitents and confessors seem aware of it or choose to use it. Perhaps the long absence of proclaiming Scripture during confessions in the past, or the sheer volume of choices in the present has dissuaded this practice from taking root.

This option derives from principles in the Constitution on the Sacred Liturgy, which said, "Sacred scripture is of the greatest importance in the celebration of the liturgy. . . . Hence, in order to achieve the restoration, progress, and adaptation of the sacred liturgy it is essential to promote that warm and lively appreciation of sacred scripture to which the

26. Sacra Congregatio pro Cultu Divino, Schemata n. 387, De Pænitentia 14, addendum III (14 February 1973), p. 2.

venerable tradition of eastern and western rites gives testimony" (24).[27]

In the early drafts, as noted above, the priest and penitent were encouraged to read from Scripture and pray together before the confession of sins. The reading moved into its own separate place in the published edition, but the drafts show how the list of passages evolved.

One draft suggested additional options from the New Testament, without offering specific citations. Some of these treated the theme of forgiveness, such as the paralytic (presumably the healing in Matt 9:1-8; Mark 2:1-12; or Luke 5:17-26); Mary Magdalene (presumably a false attribution conflating her with the sinful woman in Luke 7:36-50); the lost son (surely Luke 15:11-32); the drachma (Luke 15:8-10); and the lost sheep (Luke 15:4-7). Other passages show the love of Christ for humanity: the First Letter of John, the second chapter of Philippians, and the Gospel of John. Still other verses show the dignity and preeminence of one's vocation, especially the letters of Paul. Such passages would show the penitent some positive categories and values of the Christian life, rather than only a sense of guilt.[28]

In another draft the penitent was invited to recite some verses of a penitential psalm, such as 51, 32, or 130. These could be coupled with a verse inspired by the gospel of the publican in the temple, "Lord Jesus, have mercy on me, a sinner" (cf. Luke 18:13). The draft required the priest, who expresses the intercession of the Church, to associate himself with the penitent's prayer of contrition.[29] He enters the confessional not only as the one who absolves, but as a fragile sinner too.

A late draft invited the priest or penitent to read one selection from a long list of biblical citations for a ritual moment

---

27. *Vatican II*, p. 127.
28. Schemata n. 251 allegatum II, p. 8.
29. Schemata n. 386, p. 12.

it called "The Proclamation of the Mercy of God."[30] The published edition kept the optional reading but removed that heading. However, its sentiment remains in the rubric that describes the purpose of this reading, announcing the mercy of God (OP 43). As will be seen, the published edition repositioned the heading toward the end of one's confession, when the priest proclaimed God's mercy just before dismissing the penitent. However, it changed the title from the proclamation of mercy to the proclamation of praise, when the penitent proclaims the enduring mercy of God (OP 47).

In the same draft, the list of options for this reading was vast. From the Old Testament: Isaiah 40:2-5, 41:8-10, 41:13-14, 52:1-2, 53:4-6, 54:6-8, 58:6-8; Jeremiah 2:12-13, 3:12, 31:31-33; Ezekiel 11:19-20, 18:24-32; or Sirach 28:2-6.[31]

From the gospels: Mark 1:14-15, 2:13-17; Matthew 5:23-24, 6:14-15, 18:15-20, 18:21-35, 21:28-32; Luke 3:10-19, 6:20-26, 6:31-38, 15:1-7, 15:11-32, 18:9-14, 19:1-10, 23:33-34a, 23:39-43, 24:46-47; and John 8:1-11, 8:31-36, 20:19-23.[32]

From the other New Testament books: Romans 5:8-9, 6:11-14, 7:18-25, 12:9-21, 13:8-14; 1 Corinthians 12:12-27, 13:1-8; 2 Corinthians 5:17-21; Ephesians 4:1-6, 5:1-2; Colossians 1:12-14, 3:1-4, 3:8-10 and 12-17; 1 John 1:6-7, 2:1-2; and Revelation 2:2-5. Priests and penitents were free to choose some other verses found in the drafts or any other passage that they considered appropriate.[33]

The penitent received the Scripture and turned to prayer with a verse such as "Have mercy on me, O God, according to your merciful love" (Ps 51:3) or "Lord Jesus, son of God, have

---

30. Schemata n. 387, p. 26.
31. Schemata n. 387, pp. 42–43.
32. Schemata n. 387, pp. 43–44.
33. Schemata n. 387, pp. 44–45.

mercy on me, a sinner."[34] The penitent could choose from another long list of options: Psalms 25:4-5, 25:6-7, 25:18, 27:8, 30:3, 30:12-13, 31:6, 31:15, 32:5, 51:4-5, 51:9-10, 51:11-12, 51:13-14, 51:17, 85:8, 85:9, 101:1, 103:2-4, 103:8-9, 103:10-13, 106:1, 130:3-4, 143:1-2. Other suggestions came from the gospels: Mark 1:10; Luke 15:18, 18:13, 18:38, 19:8; and John 6:69-70. The draft permitted the penitent to choose some other passage.[35]

The same drafts invited the priest and penitent to pray together, reciting some verses of a psalm, saying a liturgical oration, or offering spontaneous words to God.[36]

When Cardinal Wojtyła saw these options, he submitted that reading from Scripture during a confession was "completely impossible" because penitents come in great numbers. He suggested having the penitents read from the gospels while standing in line awaiting their turn.[37]

One draft offered a litany to Christ. The penitent would pray, "Have mercy on me," in response to each of its phrases:

> O Christ the Savior, who carried the lost sheep on your shoulders back to the sheepfold,
>
> who forgave the woman her many sins because she also loved much,
>
> who absolved the apostle Peter, who wept over his denial,
>
> who promised paradise to the contrite thief on the cross,
>
> who died because of our sins and rose for our justification,
>
> who sits at the right hand of God the Father, ever living to intercede for us.[38]

---

34. Schemata n. 386, p. 21; and Schemata n. 387, p. 26.
35. Schemata n. 387, pp. 45–47.
36. Schemata n. 386, pp. 21–22; and Schemata n. 387, p. 27.
37. Schemata n. 387 addendum III, p. 14.
38. Schemata n. 387, p. 47.

It also offered sample penitential prayers to which the penitent answered, "Amen":

> Let your mercy, O Lord, come upon us, we pray, and may all our iniquities be wiped away by your swift indulgence. Through Christ our Lord.
>
> Hear the prayers of supplicants, we pray, O Lord, and spare those confessing their sins to you, that in your kindness you may equally grant us indulgence and peace. Through Christ our Lord.
>
> Kindly absolve us from all sins, O Lord, that, after we sinners receive your pardon, we may serve you with minds set free. Through Christ our Lord.
>
> Draw near to our supplications, O Lord, remove not your mercy from your servants, heal our wounds and forgive our sins, that, no longer separated from you by iniquities, we may ever cling to you, the Lord. Through Christ our Lord.[39]

The published edition set aside these proposed preliminary litanies and prayers. The reading of Scripture became optional, and the choice of passage fell to the priest, though penitents could read one of their own choosing. After the reading, the response of the penitent also disappeared.

These introductory rituals presume a widespread knowledge among Catholics that they should enter the confessional, hear the priest welcome them, lead the sign of the cross, let the priest invite them to trust in God, respond, "Amen," and listen in case the priest cites a passage from the Bible, or read one of their own choosing. This rarely happens, but ever since 1974 The Order of Penance has envisioned that all of that takes place before the penitent begins to confess.

39. Schemata n. 387, p. 48.

The Confession of Sins and the Acceptance of Satisfaction

More commonly, the penitent enters the confessional and starts with the words, "Bless me, Father, for I have sinned." Catechists and parents have taught these words to children and to adults. The formula has entered the culture.

It appears nowhere in The Order of Penance.

Every so often the liturgical books demonstrate a disconnection with popular culture, and this marks a clear case. Another example is the sign of the cross that many Catholics make after receiving communion or while hearing the priest's blessing at the end of Mass. Both signs are absent from the Missal.

General Formula

In truth, the rubrics say that the penitent states a general formula of confession where this is customary (OP 44). However, the given example is the *Confiteor* from the Order of Mass ("I confess to almighty God . . ."). Saying "Bless me, Father" is not contrary to the rubrics, even though the words are completely missing. The penitent may make the declaration as a general formula of sinfulness before naming specific sins. But there are other options, including the omission of that formula altogether.

In a sense, the priest's earlier invitation to trust usurps the sinner's classic request. The priest has just prayed that the light, the Lord, or the grace of the Holy Spirit may enter the penitent's heart (OP 42, 69, 70). Even before the penitent can ask, "Bless me, Father," the ritual has the priest saying words of blessing. If the priest has given the invitation to trust, the penitent is incongruently requesting a blessing that just happened.

The members of the study group traced the origins of the formula, "Bless me, Father, for I have sinned," to a sixteenth-century Cistercian Ritual. They also sought more expressive words for the penitent to say, such as "Bless me, Father, that I may obtain pardon for my sins."[40] Such a formula would move beyond a self-referential acknowledgment of the sinful condition to the grace-filled purpose of seeking the priest's blessing. Neither the original formula nor this proposed revision entered the published edition.

The *Confiteor* remained an option throughout the drafts, but one draft suggested a change to the second part of the prayer in order to request pardon. After confessing "I have greatly sinned . . . in what I have failed to do," the penitent could add a request to the priest, for example, "and I ask of you that you help and absolve me."[41] This suggestion likewise did not move forward.

Confession

Commonly, the penitent will tell the priest how much time has elapsed since the previous confession. The rubrics do not include this nor require it. In the Hispanic community, few penitents offer this information, and many would not know the answer if the priest requested it.

As noted above, the previous ritual had the priest ask this among other questions concerning the penitent's state of life, accuracy of the previous confession, and the fulfillment of its penance.[42] The present ritual omits all these particulars, even the information about the length of time since the previous confession. Penitents may offer whatever they judge helpful for the priest to know.

Often it does help the priest if the penitent discloses the amount of time that has elapsed. A person who confessed a week ago is different from one who last confessed twenty-five

---

40. Schemata n. 251 allegatum II, p. 3, citing *Rituale Cisterciense*, Liber III, Caput IX, and other sources.

41. Schemata n. 251 allegatum II, p. 3.

42. *Rituale Romanum*, Titulus IV, Caput I:12, p. 131.

years ago. A married person with children is different from a single or recently divorced person. A person active in a parish is different from one who rarely gets involved. The penitent may judge what feels apt to share.

The priest may help penitents articulate their sins. He may offer advice. He urges contrition. He recalls that through this sacrament the penitent personally participates in the paschal mystery of the death and resurrection of Christ (OP 44). This provides one example of how the theme of the paschal mystery, so close to the postconciliar liturgical renewal, emanates from each of the sacraments and applies them to the lives of the faithful. As the Constitution on the Sacred Liturgy says, "for well-disposed members of the faithful, the liturgy of the sacraments and sacramentals sanctifies almost every event of their lives with the divine grace which flows from the paschal mystery of the passion, death and resurrection of Christ. From this source all sacraments and sacramentals draw their power" (61).[43]

These instructions for the priest simplify the ones from before the Council, which also called for a general confession such as the *Confiteor* before listing individual sins. The former ritual urged the priest to listen to the entire confession and only ask for more information if needed to elicit the complete acknowledgment of one's sins.[44] That advice still pertains.

Concerning the confessing of sins, the present ritual says surprisingly little, especially given that most people know this sacrament as "confession." It simply instructs the penitent to confess (OP 44). Each one may choose how to do this. If the penitent has prepared through a good examination of conscience, its fruit will be clear. Some penitents have only a few sins that are bothering them; others offer a cascading litany of offenses. Some adults read the sins that they have tapped onto their cell phones. Some children at their first confession recite

---

43. *Vatican II*, p. 139.
44. *Rituale Romanum*, Titulus IV, Caput I:16, p. 132.

a well-prepared list of sins; others freeze under the anxiety of the moment. The priest may lend reasonable assistance.

Priests are used to hearing a variety of approaches to the enumeration of sins. Penitents need not worry overmuch about doing this in a certain way.

Work of Penance

The priest proposes a work of penance through which each penitent makes satisfaction for their sins and amends their life. The Order of Penance says both that the priest imposes a penance (18) and proposes a penance (44). The discrepancy suggests some lack of clarity. Does the priest decide on the penance alone, or does the penitent get to approve it? If the work assigned seems too difficult, the penitent would do well to inform the priest and request something else. The priest may do well to ask the penitent if the penance is acceptable. That can avoid a situation where the penitent has to confess incompletion of the assigned penance at a future confession. The penance may be prayer, an act of self-denial, or especially service to one's neighbor, which underscores the social aspect of sin and forgiveness (18).

The penance is not a commensurate sentence. It is not a punishment equal to the crime. It is an expression of one's intent to reform one's life. It has more to do with future behavior, not with past sin.

In drafting the imposition of the penance, one idea was to create a formula with which the priest would solemnly begin: "And now, to show your contrition before God and the Church, do these things."[45] The priest would thus have explicitly declared the need for contrition and its connection to the work of penance.

In another draft, before imposing a penance, the priest offered appropriate counsel and then exhorted the penitent

---

45. Schemata n. 251 allegatum II, p. 4.

toward contrition, looking to Jesus (Heb 12:2), who loved and gave himself up for the sinner (Gal 2:20). He encouraged the penitent to die and rise in Christ, being renewed in the paschal mystery.[46]

One draft proposed a conclusion to the imposition of the penance. The priest would say "May the almighty and merciful Lord grant you a time of true and fruitful penitence, an ever-penitent heart and correction of life, the grace and consolation of the Holy Spirit, and perseverance to the end." The penitent would respond, "Amen."[47] The revisers relied on a variety of sources for this formula, including the Holy Thursday Reconciliation of Penitents from the appendix of the Roman Pontifical and the solemn papal blessing. They intended to express the necessary dispositions of each penitent to amend their life. Indeed, the revisers thought that such a formula would have diminished the need for the penitent to recite an act of contrition, and that it would have stressed the role of the community, represented by the priest interceding for the sinner's conversion.[48]

Another draft gave the priest this alternative: "May God free you from every evil and save you in his heavenly kingdom: to him be glory for ever." To which the penitent would answer, "Amen."[49]

In the end, no formula accompanies the assignment of the penance. The improvisatory nature of a confession continues through this part of the liturgy. Indeed, the priest is reminded to adapt his manner of speaking and his counsel to the circumstances of each penitent (OP 44). He needs to respond immediately and uniquely to each penitent, no matter their age, intelligence, or spiritual maturity.

---

46. Schemata n. 386, p. 22.
47. Schemata n. 251 allegatum II, p. 4.
48. Schemata n. 265, p. 4.
49. Schemata n. 361, p. 48.

The Prayer of the Penitent

The Act of Contrition

The priest invites the penitent to express contrition, and the penitent offers a prayer. Because the published edition did not import the idea from the drafts that the priest and penitent would pray together before the confession of sins, this remains the only moment in the confession when anyone addresses God directly. The role falls to the penitent, as did the sign of the cross at the beginning of the confession. This contrasts with the role of the priest at Mass, where he is responsible for articulating most of the prayers on behalf of the assembly. Here, the penitent alone addresses God. In this prayer the penitent admits their personal sin and resolves to amend their life (OP 45).

The "prayer of the penitent" is more commonly known as the "act of contrition." In this setting, the word "act" represents a declaration of an interior disposition. It occupies a category with other traditional prayers such as an "act of faith," "of hope," and "of love." Although the act of contrition follows a common contour, Catholics have learned a variety of specific formulas. The revised translation offers yet another version of this popular prayer. The penitent may use similar words—composing a prayer that expresses contrition and a resolution to amend. Or the penitent may choose from the wide selection of prayers in OP 85–92.

Revising Previous Expressions of Contrition

In the Roman Ritual before the Council, the *Confiteor* served as the prayer of the penitent. It did not follow the confession of sins, but preceded it. An early draft of the revision omitted the *Confiteor*.[50] The revisers then explained several reasons for this: the *Confiteor* concerned a single personal confession,

50. Schemata n. 265, p. 2.

rather than the communitarian dimensions of sin; many penitents did not know the formula; the requirement to recite it created artificiality; it raised the danger of merely mouthing the words; and it was already in use in other venues, such as the penitential act of the Mass.[51]

Formulas for the act of contrition have circulated at least since the tenth-century Roman-Germanic Pontifical, where penitents began a confession with a prayer of sorrow before the bishop quizzed them on dozens of potential offenses. Because a variety of formulas for the act of contrition evolved over the centuries, the study group recommended copying the *Confiteor* exactly from the Order of Mass if it was to remain here.[52]

As the drafts progressed, they offered the penitent options for this prayer before confessing sin: verses from Psalm 51; invocations inspired by the gospel, such as "Lord Jesus, have mercy on me, a sinner"; verses from a penitential psalm, such as 32, 51, or 130; some liturgical text or an improvised prayer.[53] The priest could join the penitent.[54]

After the confession, the late drafts called for the priest and penitent to recite the Lord's Prayer together, the priest also being a sinner in need of the mercy of God. "In this way, he who is the father, the healer of souls, and the minister of reconciliation, shows himself also a brother to his visitor entreating the mercy of God."[55] The priest was to introduce the Lord's Prayer in these or similar words: "Let us ask God the Father to have mercy on us sinners, saying together the prayer that Christ himself taught us."[56]

51. Schemata n. 267, p. 3.
52. Schemata n. 272, p. 24, citing the Roman-Germanic Pontifical CXXXVI:2–3.
53. Schemata n. 386, p. 12.
54. Schemata n. 387, p. 13.
55. Schemata n. 386, p. 12; Schemata n. 387, p. 14.
56. Schemata n. 386, p. 22; Schemata n. 387, p. 27.

The revisers considered the Lord's Prayer important for obtaining reconciliation with God and with one's brothers and sisters. "The penitent, as the prodigal son, approaches God and proclaims the necessity of the coming kingdom of God, asks that his will be done, affirms the connection between the pardon requested from God and the pardon given by the rest of us, and prays that God will free us from temptation and evil."[57]

The proposal to add the Lord's Prayer to a confession met some opposition from consultors. Some liked it, but only as an option. Pope Paul VI sent an intervention through Cardinal Jean-Marie Villot:

> The Lord's Prayer does not seem an appropriate prayer to manifest the contrition and purpose demanded of the sacrament of reconciliation. It would rather need "an act of contrition and purpose" more directly expressive and relative to the conversion proper to this sacrament. In the event that one would not want to compose a new fitting act of contrition, one could find in the psalter and the gospels some appropriate, brief, and well-known verses, but explicitly relative to repentance, to the request for pardon, to the appeal for mercy, and to conversion of heart, as all the penitential literature seems to affirm (see Luke 15:13, Ps 51, St. Ambrose "On Penance" II:VII,53).[58]

Cardinal Villot offered other examples, including the prayer of St. Ambrose before Mass: "Be mindful, O Lord, of the one you have created, whom you have redeemed by your blood. It pains me to have sinned; I desire to correct what I have done. Take away from me, most compassionate Father, all iniquities and all my sins; so that, having been purified in mind and body, I may be fit to worthily taste the most holy

57. Schemata n. 386, p. 13.
58. Schemata n. 387 addendum III, p. 15.

things." Villot also proposed a choice of one of the first four prayers from the Litany of the Saints.[59]

In the end, the *Confiteor* remained one option for the general confession of sins, though many penitents replace it with the formula, "Bless me, Father, for I have sinned." The prayer of the penitent moved from its position before confessing to a position after confessing, and the Lord's Prayer was removed from the individual confession of sins.

Options for the Prayer of the Penitent

For the prayer of the penitent, the revised translation offers a clean, understandable formula (OP 45). However, as with any revision, a change makes it harder to memorize anew. Penitents may bring a copy with them, view one on their cellular device, read from copies provided in the confessional, recite the version they already have memorized, or compose their own.

The act of contrition expresses sorrow for sins of commission and of omission. That is, the penitent repents of wrongful things done and of good opportunities forsaken. The penitent expresses the reason for this sorrow: offense against God, who is all good and worthy to be loved more than anything else, even the transitory pleasures that sin temptingly provides.

Absent from the reasons for contrition is a phrase that some versions of the prayer included: "because I fear the loss of heaven and the pains of hell." That expression presumed that all sins committed and confessed were grave, putting one's salvation out of reach and ensuring eternal damnation. Not all sins are that grave, so the act of contrition in The Order of Penance does not make that assumption.

The penitent concludes the act of contrition by resolving with God's grace to do penance, stop sinning, and even to avoid occasions for sinning. The prayer concludes with a re-

59. Schemata n. 387 addendum III, p. 15.

quest for mercy that the passion of Jesus Christ makes possible. This conclusion again fulfills one aim of the revision, to keep the paschal mystery of the death and resurrection of Christ ever before the penitent.

The penitent may substitute another prayer, and The Order of Penance supplies several beautiful examples (85–92). The first three of these come directly from the Scriptures (Ps 25:6-7; Ps 51:4-5; Luke 15:18, 18:13).

Another is based on the accounts of the prodigal son and the good thief, while calling on the Holy Spirit, the fount of love, a title taken from the sequence *Veni, Creator* (OP 88). Another example recalls the many healings of Jesus and his forgiveness of the sinful woman (refreshingly no longer assumed to be Mary Magdalene) and of Peter. In it the penitent also asks to live in communion with others, capturing the communitarian dimension of reconciliation so desired by the revision (OP 89).

Another possible prayer of the penitent is asking for freedom from sin through the death and resurrection of Christ, echoing again the paschal mystery (OP 90). One more is to call Jesus the Lamb of God who takes away the sin of the world (John 1:29), and in whose blood the penitent is washed clean (Rev 7:14). It also invokes the grace of the Holy Spirit, whose role the revision underscored (OP 91).

Order of Penance 92 offers two options. The first recalls the spirit of Psalm 51:11-12, and the second, and briefest of all the suggestions, is the popular "Jesus prayer," inspired by Jesus' parable of the tax collector in the temple area (Luke 18:13). Perhaps it was added as an afterthought and placed here as an alternative, a solution that avoids renumbering all the remaining paragraphs.

Apparently for a similar reason, the edition in the United States adds a third option to Order of Penance 92, a popular rendering of the act of contrition. It differs from the one in the main section of the ritual (OP 45) by listing God's "just punishments" as an additional motive for repentance. It also specifies a resolution to avoid "near occasions" of sin instead of "occasions" of sin. This recovers traditional vocabulary, like the word "detest" earlier in the prayer, and does not aim to limit the occasions one intends to avoid.

Making these prayers available to penitents may enrich the quality of their contrition and intent, immerse them more deeply in the Scriptures, and help them apply a specific prayer to the spirit of repentance they experience in the sacrament actually being celebrated.

Special Circumstances: Absolution from Censures

In its first appendix, The Order of Penance includes a treatment of special circumstances that are to be resolved when reconciling certain individuals. These pertain to sins that incur a canonical penalty, but their forgiveness implies a liturgical act.

Priests and penitents may largely be unaware of the ritual implications of these circumstances, but The Order of Penance wraps them inside the book. Occupying only a single page, this brief appendix masks the magnitude of its results. It returns an unusually grave sinner to renewed life in the Christian community. It demonstrates the greatness of God's mercy for the sinner who repents.

The Code of Canon Law lists a number of offenses that incur automatic penalties. These include such sins as adopting a heresy (canon 1364 §1), using a consecrated host for a sacrilegious purpose (1382), procuring an abortion (1397), absolving an accomplice in a sexual sin (1384), attempting to ordain a woman (1379 §3), feigning priesthood by attempting to celebrate Mass or give absolution (1379 §1 1°, 2°), attacking a bishop (1370 §2), or aiding someone in accomplishing such actions. The offense may incur interdict, which prohibits participation in some forms of worship (915; 1332); excommunication, which further prohibits participation in some forms of governance (1331);

and suspension, which prohibits clergy from performing some functions of the office that they hold (1333–1335).

In some circumstances a priest may absolve a person from a censure outside the sacrament of penance. In that case, The Order of Penance supplies a formula (Appendix I:2). Within the sacrament of penance, the regular formula of absolution suffices if the confessor intends it to include release from censures (Appendix I:1). For example, a penitent who confesses an abortion, which incurs an automatic excommunication (canon 1397 §2), is forgiven with the usual words of absolution when the priest intends to remove the censure. Or the priest may offer the explicit absolution from excommunication found in this appendix before reciting the usual formula.

Absolution

The Gesture

As he gives absolution, the priest extends his hands over the penitent's head—or at least raises his right hand (OP 46). The gesture has a long history.

St. Cyprian (†258) remarked that the bishop or some member of the clergy imposed a hand as one sign of reconciliation at public gatherings.[60] By the Middle Ages, when penitents confessed anonymously in private, the imposition of hands known from antiquity became less important, as the penitent would not have seen it. Thomas Aquinas (†1274) argued that no prayer was necessary, nor any external gesture, but only the words, "I absolve you."[61] In his view the sacrament was not aimed toward obtaining some excellence of grace, but toward the forgiveness of sins.[62]

---

60. Schemata n. 272, p. 8.

61. Schemata n. 272, p. 27, citing IV. d.22 q.2 a.2 sol. 3, and "On the Form of Absolution" 3 q.84 a.3.

62. Schemata n. 272, p. 27, citing III. q.84 a.4.

The Roman Ritual of 1614 reintroduced raising the right hand toward the penitent. Because the ritual required a grille to separate the priest and the penitent, the gesture seemed useless from the perspective of the penitent, who never would have seen it. Because the gesture was not required for validity, some confessors omitted it. The revisers wanted to reinstate the imposition of hands because of the antiquity of the gesture and its appropriateness for signifying an outpouring of divine grace, without which no forgiveness of sins happens. They proposed that the priest extend both hands toward the penitent instead of the more traditional imposition of hands, so that the gesture required no physical contact. They permitted the priest to raise only his right hand as an alternative because an extension of his hands would not be possible in all cases, such as in the confessional or in some public venue requiring more anonymity.[63]

After the drafts had proposed this gesture, consultors offered commentary. Pierre-Marie Gy, for example, recommended that in absolving women, priests should raise one hand, rather than impose both.[64] Balthasar Fischer advocated extending both hands while sitting, because judges in antiquity sat to impose a judgment, or imposing both hands while standing over the penitent.[65]

A late draft had the priest impose the penance either sitting or standing. The penitent, who may have been seated, was to stand, kneel, or bow to receive absolution. The priest imposed hands on the head of the penitent or at least raised his right hand; the draft preferred the imposition of hands with which the apostles healed the sick, expelled demons, and conferred the Holy Spirit.[66] In commentary on this proposal, Jacques

---

63. Schemata n. 272, p. 27; Schemata n. 361, pp. 31–32.
64. Schemata n. 267, p. 1.
65. Schemata n. 267, pp. 1–2.
66. Schemata n. 387, p. 14.

Lahache thought it was one of the most striking symbols of reconciliation with God, but Cyril Papali thought the option of imposing hands should be removed because it was impossible when hearing the confessions of women, who had to confess their sins behind a grille. Cardinal Wojtyła wanted the gesture removed because it would make it hard to maintain secrecy over the decision to bestow or deny absolution: an outsider could tell by looking whether or not the penitent had been absolved. Cardinal John Cody called it unrealistic to expect that these new details would be followed in the modern day.[67]

In the end, the ritual calls for the priest to extend hands over the penitent's head as the first option, which presumes that the confession is taking place face-to-face, not behind a grille. The second option is for him to extend his right hand (OP 46). The placing of hands directly on the head of the penitent is not mentioned.

The Revised Translation

The words of absolution have a revised English translation with only a few minor changes—just enough to make it hard to memorize correctly. Instead of "sent the Holy Spirit among us," the words are "poured out the Holy Spirit." This closer translation of the Latin original probably alludes to Romans 5:5: "the love of God has been poured out into our hearts through the holy Spirit that has been given to us." The words "among us" were added into the first English translation, but the outpouring of the Spirit in this case is more individualized.

Instead of "give," the word has become "grant." This probably aims to bestow a resonance of great and undeserved generosity.

There are also changes to the conventions of capitalization: "Death" and "Resurrection," when referring to those of Christ, now carry capital letters in the liturgical books, and sacramental

67. Schemata 387 addendum III, pp. 15–16.

formulas appear with small caps. None of these changes significantly affects the meaning of absolution, and few penitents will likely take notice of these few syllables. No one, of course, will hear capital letters. If a priest accidentally reverts to the previous formula, it will not affect the bestowal of valid absolution.

The word "God" appears twice in the revised English translation, as was true in the first one, even though the word appears only once in Latin. The second instance, "may God grant you pardon and peace," seems important for the sake of clarity. Without it, it could sound to English-speakers as if the priest were asking pardon and peace from the Holy Spirit, rather than from the Father.

History

History reflects many changes to the words of absolution, so the postconciliar discussion about revising them was understandably lively and complex. The previous form of absolution, found in the Roman Ritual, comprised five sections, all delivered in Latin.[68] The first resembles words currently part of the penitential act in the Order of Mass (4): "May almighty God have mercy on you, forgive you your sins, and bring you to everlasting life. Amen." These words appear as early as the tenth-century Roman-Germanic Pontifical as part of the ceremony for the order of penitents on Ash Wednesday.[69]

In the second section, the priest said, "May the almighty and merciful Lord grant you pardon, absolution and forgiveness of your sins. Amen." These words, according to Josef Andreas Jungmann, came from the thirteenth-century Pontifical of Durandus in the ceremony for reconciling penitents on Holy Thursday.[70]

---

68. *Rituale Romanum*, Titulus IV, Caput II:1–3, pp. 134–35.

69. Schemata n. 222, p. 6, citing *Le Pontifical Romano-Germanique du Dixième Siècle*, vol. 2, ed. Cyrille Vogel and Reinhard Elze, *Studi e Testi* 226 (Vatican City: Biblioteca Apostolica Vaticana, 1963), p. 17.

70. Schemata n. 222, p. 6.

In the third section, the priest said, "May our Lord Jesus Christ absolve you; and by his authority I absolve you from every bond of excommunication, suspension, and interdict, insofar as I am able and you have need." The study group cited the 1584 Ritual of Cardinal Giulio Antonio Santori as the source. The revisers acknowledged a problem with this section: The words "from every bond of excommunication" originally meant that the person was readmitted to the ecclesiastical communion from which sin had gravely separated the penitent. According to current law, the words "in no way suffice for removing excommunication in the modern sense."[71]

The fourth section opens with the Latin word for "Then," which the revisers understood as a rubrical note added to the spoken text in the seventeenth century to give what follows some grandeur. The priest was "then" to say the words, "I absolve you from your sins in the name of the Father, and of the Son, ✝ and of the Holy Spirit." Aquinas maintained that this indicative formula (stating what the priest was doing), which was fairly recent in his day, was necessary for validity. However, certain manuscripts show the valid usage of other types of formulas. Some were deprecative (praying to God) and others declarative (declaring what God was doing), and were in use beyond the days of Aquinas up to the fourteenth century.[72]

In the final section, the priest said words that formed the basis of what became an optional concluding formula in the revision (OP 93), "May the passion of our Lord Jesus Christ, the merits of the Blessed Virgin Mary and of all the saints, whatever good you do and evil you endure, be for you forgiveness of your sins, bring you an increase of grace and the reward of eternal life." The revisers traced this to the fifteenth-century

---

71. Schemata n. 222, p. 6.

72. Schemata n. 222, p. 6, citing the opusculum "On the Form of Absolution," 3 q.84 a.3.

Penitential of Vallicella II. Earlier, Aquinas had already recommended the second part of this section.[73]

Reviewing these five elements, the revisers raised questions about the preconciliar formula of absolution. The repetitions seemed without benefit. Certain words did not relate to the modern reality and were poorly understood (probably referring to "excommunication"). The formula said nothing about the role of the Church itself in the reconciliation of the sinner. The group considered diverse solutions: keeping the substantial formula in force, with necessary modifications; devising a new formula from the rich heritage of antiquity in Latin and Eastern traditions; or pose several formulas from which the confessor could choose, including a modified version of the one then in force.[74] This last solution allowed the revisers to consider giving the confessor a choice among alternative formulas based on the historically diverse indicative, deprecative, and declarative types.

Proposed Revisions

The revisers initially proposed this formula: "Our Lord Jesus Christ, who by his passion and resurrection redeemed the sins of the world, through me, an unworthy minister of his Church, absolves you from all your sins." The penitent answered, "Amen" or "Thanks be to God."[75] This changed the indicative formula concerning the priest's action to a declarative one concerning the action of the Lord Jesus Christ. The formula also made Christ the one who absolves, rather than the priest. In fact, it reduced the priest to the rank of "unworthy minister." It introduced elements of the paschal mystery (passion, resurrection, and redemption).

The proposed revision provoked many comments: Rahner and Anciaux wanted reconciliation with the Church to be

73. Schemata n. 222, p. 6, citing Quodlibetal Questions 3, q.13 a.28.
74. Schemata n. 222, p. 6.
75. Schemata n. 251 allegatum II, p. 5.

clearer. Several wanted a deprecative formula, a prayer addressed to God. Some wanted mention of the power to forgive sins that Christ gave the apostles, an element in other historic forms of absolution. Some still wanted several formulas from which the priest could choose one.[76]

The group reviewed points from an important treasury of prayers concerning reconciliation, the Roman Pontifical's centuries-old rite for reconciling penitents on Holy Thursday.[77] Concerning the formula of absolution, the revisers noted, the only one from the Pontifical was neither indicative nor declarative, but deprecative.[78]

Among other prayers preceding absolution in the ancient ceremony, several reveal theological insights that almost prophetically addressed the contemporary desire to stress the penitent's reconciliation with the Church. The first example comes from the "preface," a term used for some lengthy prayers led by the bishop even outside of Mass. In this instance, he prayed that God would regather the repentant sinners "into the bosom of your Church."[79]

Subsequent prayers asked that sinners "be returned guiltless to your holy Church," and "restored to the holy altars," "lest your holy Church be devastated in any portion of its body, lest your flock endure loss, lest the enemy exult over the damnation of your family."[80] More prayers asked, "Rejoin the redeemed portion to the unity of the body of the Church," "so that, having received a wedding garment, they may be made worthy to enter the royal table, from which they had been expelled."[81]

76. Schemata n. 251 allegatum II, p. 5.
77. Schemata n. 251 allegatum II, pp. 5–6.
78. *Pontificale Romanum, Editio Princeps (1595–1596),* 572–73.
79. *Pontificale (1595–1596),* p. 567.
80. *Pontificale (1595–1596),* p. 571.
81. *Pontificale (1595–1596),* p. 572.

Absolution in the same Holy Thursday ritual connected some themes that some of the revisers sought to include: the power given to the apostles and the causality of the blood of Christ. A revision of that ancient prayer supplied the next idea for the new words of absolution:

> May our Lord Jesus Christ, who was pleased to purge the sins of the whole world by the outpouring of his blood, and who conferred onto his disciples the power of forgiving sins, absolve you, by my ministry, from all your sins, and be pleased to reconnect the redeemed portion, freed from the bond of sins, to the unity of the body of the Church. Who lives and reigns.[82]

In time, this was also revised, eliminating the reference to Christ's blood and restoring a simpler acknowledgment of his suffering drawn from the same original prayer. The concluding phrase seemed unclear even in Latin, so the group adopted a simpler ending:

> May our Lord Jesus Christ, who was pleased to purge the sins of the whole world by his betrayal, and who conferred onto his disciples the power of forgiving sins, absolve you, by my ministry, from all your sins, and restore you through complete forgiveness to the unity of his Church. Who lives and reigns.[83]

The penitent responded, "Amen." The same draft finally proposed alternative forms of absolution to that first option, giving the priest a choice. The second simplified the initial revised formula:

> Our Lord Jesus Christ, who by his passion and resurrection redeemed the sins of the world, absolves you

82. Schemata n. 251 allegatum II, p. 6.
83. Schemata n. 265, p. 2.

from your sins and restores you fully into the peace of
the Church.[84]

The group amplified this declarative form to include the
ecclesial dimension of reconciliation. It also removed the
humble acknowledgment of the priest's unworthiness.
The third option was based on the traditional formula:

> May the Lord Jesus Christ absolve you, and by his au-
> thority I absolve you from your sins in the name of the
> Father and of the Son and of the Holy Spirit.[85]

The minister could then add the next section from the
Roman Ritual, "May the passion . . . " The penitent answered, "Amen," to each of these statements.[86] This revision
expressed the background for the priest's statement, "I absolve
you," by saying first that the Lord Jesus Christ absolves and
gives the priest authority to do the same.

The last option comes directly from one of the Pontifical's
prayers over all the penitents on Holy Thursday just before
absolving the group. The revisers rendered it in the singular,
as it appeared in the eighth-century Gelasian Sacramentary,[87]
and repurposed it as absolution itself:

> Grant, we pray, O Lord, to this your servant the worthy
> fruit of penitence, so that, by obtaining pardon from
> errors, he (she) may be returned guiltless to your holy
> Church from whose unity he (she) had wandered by
> sinning.[88]

84. Schemata n. 265, pp. 2–3.
85. Schemata n. 265, p. 3.
86. Schemata n. 265, p. 3.
87. *Liber Sacramentorum Romanæ Æclesiæ Ordinis Anni Circuli (Sacra-
mentarium Gelasianum)*, ed. Leo Cunibert Mohlberg (Rome: Casa Editrice
Herder, 1981), n. 357.
88. Schemata n. 265, p. 3. See *Pontificale (1595–1596)*, p. 571.

These ideas elicited even more suggestions. Anciaux wanted an explicit mention of the work of the Holy Spirit in the reconciliation of a sinner.[89] Bishop Alfred Pichler wanted a formula more biblical than juridical, one that named the paschal mystery as the source of grace. He also favored the indicative form ("I absolve") over the deprecative form, which addresses the Lord, and which he thought belonged among alternatives. Bishop Guilford Young wanted to stress the ecclesial nature of the sacrament, and Cardinal Michele Pellegrino favored a mention of the increase of grace that the sacrament effects.[90]

The key section of the five-part form of absolution in force used the words "I absolve you from your sins" in the name of the Trinity. Though defended by Aquinas for its validity, the revisers considered the formula extremely poor given the Council's desires for the renewal of this rite. It failed to answer expectations of the Constitution on the Sacred Liturgy because it was not sufficiently biblical, it did not express clearly the nature and effect of the sacrament, nor did it show the ecclesial and communitarian aspects, nor make mention of the action of the Holy Spirit.[91] Therefore, the group again revised the first of its formulas:

> May our Lord Jesus Christ, who was pleased to free the whole world by his betrayal, and who conferred onto his disciples the power of forgiving sins, absolve you, by my ministry, from all your sins, and restore you by the grace of his Spirit to the perfect unity of the Church. Who lives and reigns.[92]

The penitent answered, "Amen." The group called the style of this formula "optative"; that is, expressing a desire that

89. Schemata n. 267, p. 1.
90. Schemata n. 272, p. 28.
91. Schemata n. 272, p. 29.
92. Schemata n. 272, p. 29.

something may happen. Although the Roman Ritual in force did not use that voice for the forgiveness of an individual penitent, it did appear in the pontifical's reconciliation of penitents on Holy Thursday, so the style was always valid. In addition, the formula showed the paschal mystery as the source of all forgiveness of sins, the power given to the Church, the work of priestly ministry, the forgiveness of sins, reconciliation with the Church, and the action of the Holy Spirit.[93]

The group also revised the second formula:

> Our Lord Jesus Christ, who by his passion and resurrection redeemed the world, absolves you by the grace of the Holy Spirit from your sins and restores you fully into the peace of the Church. Who lives and reigns.[94]

The penitent answered, "Amen." The revisers called this formula "declarative"—that is, it describes what the Lord does. Although the style was new to this sacrament, the Council of Florence declared valid a similar formula for baptismal liturgies. This revision expresses the forgiveness of sins and its source (the paschal mystery), the grace of the Holy Spirit, reconciliation with the Church, and—implicitly, by the action of the minister—the power given to the Church.[95]

The third formula remained unchanged, complete with the option of adding the prayer about the passion of Christ.

> May the Lord Jesus Christ absolve you, and by his authority I absolve you from your sins in the name of the Father and of the Son and of the Holy Spirit.[96]

---

93. Schemata n. 272, p. 30.

94. Schemata n. 272, p. 30.

95. Schemata n. 272, pp. 30–31, citing *Enchiridion symbolorum, definitionum et declarationum de rebus fidei et morum*, ed. Heinrich Denziger and Adolf Schönmetzer (Barcelona: Herder, 1965), 1314.

96. Schemata n. 272, p. 31.

Abbreviated from the formula in the ritual then in force, it retained only the essential elements. It was optative in the first part, "May the Lord Jesus absolve," and declarative in the second part, "I absolve," to which the penitent answered, "Amen," and the priest had the option of adding the prayer from the final section of the Roman Ritual:

> May the passion of our Lord Jesus Christ, the merits of Blessed Mary ever Virgin and of all the saints, whatever good you do and evil you endure, be for you forgiveness of your sins, bring you an increase of grace and the reward of eternal life.[97]

The repetition of the verb "absolve" seemed problematic, as if the absolutions were twofold. However, the third section of the absolution formula then in force used a similar construction. The revisers also thought that the prayer about the passion of Christ could have sufficed for absolution if enriched by a change from the "merits" of the saints to their "intercession" and by the addition of the intercession of "the whole Church." The revisers did not propose suppressing the formula in force; after all, the Councils of Florence and Trent had prescribed it. Still, they hoped that the full Consilium would keep an open mind on adjusting these formulas.[98]

The fourth option, the one from the Gelasian Sacramentary, also remained unchanged:

> Grant, we pray, O Lord, to this your servant the worthy fruit of penitence, so that, by obtaining pardon from errors, he (she) may be returned guiltless to your holy Church from whose unity he (she) had wandered by sinning.[99]

---

97. *Schemata* n. 272, p. 31.
98. *Schemata* n. 272, p. 31.
99. *Schemata* n. 272, p. 32.

Its form was deprecative—that is, it was a prayer addressed to the Lord. It restored a style used throughout the first millennium, along with a few optative formulas. The revisers thought that this option best explained the relationship between one's penance and the sacrament. It also expressed the forgiveness of sins, reconciliation with the Church, and the intercession of the Church on behalf of the sinner. The group anticipated that the translation would be problematic and suggested instead of "from whose unity he (she) had wandered by sinning," expressions from other formulas be used: "into the perfect unity of the Church" or "into the peace of the Church." They hoped that the translations would be executed with sufficient freedom so as not to confuse the state of one's sin with the state of excommunication in the modern sense.[100]

Within a couple of months the group received and responded to feedback. It emended the optative first form as follows:

> May our Lord Jesus Christ, who offered himself to the Father by sacrificing for us, and who conferred onto his Church the power of forgiving sins, himself absolve you by the grace of the Holy Spirit from your sins, and restore you into the perfect peace of the Church. Who lives and reigns.[101]

Where the previous versions mentioned the historical betrayal of Jesus, this one presents its meaning: his self-offering to the Father for the sake of the world. This version also clarified the belief that Jesus gave the power to forgive sins not only to his disciples, but to his Church. It removed the reference to the priest's own ministry of mediation. It showed that the Holy Spirit was the agent of absolution, not only of

100. Schemata n. 272, p. 32.
101. Schemata n. 279 bis, p. 2.

restoration. All of this restored the sinner not to the unity of the Church, but to its peace.

The group also revised the second formula, which is declarative, stating that Jesus Christ forgives:

> Our Lord Jesus Christ, who by his passion and resurrection redeemed the world, forgives your sins through my ministry by the grace of the Holy Spirit and restores you into the full life of the Church. Who lives and reigns.[102]

The revision removed the word "absolves" in favor of "forgives." The revisers inserted a phrase about the agency of the minister, a subject that they removed from the first option. In the revision the penitent finds restoration into the full life of the Church, instead of into its peace.

The third formula, which had thus far been indicative and juridical ("I absolve you"), changed to adopt more elements from the second:

> Our Lord Jesus Christ forgives you your sins by my ministry and restores you fully into the peace of the Church, who lives and reigns with the Father and the Holy Spirit for ever and ever.[103]

The penitent added, "Amen," and the priest had the option of adding the prayer about the passion of the Lord. This version thus also became declarative, putting the role of the minister in a prepositional phrase instead of the main verb. It introduced the ecclesial element of restoration following forgiveness.

The revisers removed the fourth option.[104] It had the longest history, dating at least to the eighth century, but it had never functioned specifically as words of absolution.

102. Schemata n. 279 bis, p. 2.
103. Schemata n. 279 bis, p. 2.
104. Schemata n. 279 bis, p. 2.

A few months later, the revisers emended the formulas again as part of a complete draft of The Order of Penance. The third option suddenly became the first option, which more nearly resembled the form of absolution from the Roman Ritual then in force. It appeared within the body of the draft:

> In the name of our Lord Jesus Christ and in the power of the Holy Spirit I absolve you from your sins and fully restore you into the peace of the Church.[105]

The penitent replied, "Amen." If it seemed appropriate, the minister continued with the prayer concerning the passion of the Lord, to which the penitent also answered, "Amen":

> May the passion of our Lord Jesus Christ, the intercession of Blessed Mary ever Virgin and of all the saints, whatever good you do and evil you endure be for you a remedy for sin, bring you an increase of grace, and the reward of eternal life.[106]

The formula used only the indicative, "I absolve you." The priest was to take his action in the name of the Lord Jesus and by the power of the Spirit. The formula retained the theme of reconciliation with the Church, specifically into the peace of the Church. The additional optional prayer changed "merits" to "intercession," as the revisers had recommended after their previous work. It also changed a word from "forgiveness" to "remedy." This version resembles an alternative that The Order of Penance offers for the proclamation of praise after absolution (OP 93).

The appendix explained that conferences of bishops could recommend other formulas that might better stress either the paschal mystery as the source of forgiveness or the ministerial work of the priest. To that end, it supplied two more alternatives.

105. Schemata n. 312, p. 5.
106. Schemata n. 312, p. 6.

The first repeated the most recent version of the one that had served as the first of all the options up to this point:

> May our Lord Jesus Christ, who offered himself to the Father by sacrificing for us, and who conferred onto his Church the power of forgiving sins, himself absolve you by the grace of the Holy Spirit from your sins, and restore you into the perfect peace of the Church. Who lives and reigns.[107]

Similarly, the final alternative repeated the formula that developed through the previous drafts as the second option. It declared the forgiveness that comes from Christ:

> Our Lord Jesus Christ, who by his passion and resurrection redeemed the world, forgives your sins through my ministry by the grace of the Holy Spirit and restores you into the full life of the Church. Who lives and reigns.[108]

After receiving feedback, the revisers explained their reasons for the two formulas supplied in the appendix. The main formula closely follows the recent tradition, in which the priest says, "I absolve you," and it includes an optional second part. The length of this double formula troubled some reviewers of the work. Some of them preferred abbreviating the main formula to its first part alone, though that would eliminate mention of the passion of Christ, the intercession of the saints, and the important cooperation of the penitent. The revisers were focused on devising a formula of absolution that best expressed its meaning.[109]

The two formulas in the appendix took a different focus: the role of Christ, the principal minister of reconciliation,

---

107. Schemata n. 312, p. 9.

108. Schemata n. 312, p. 9.

109. Consilium ad Exsequendam Constitutionem de Sacra Liturgia, Schemata n. 350, De Pænitentia 10 (23 September 1969), p. 1.

and the cooperation of the priest in his ministerial role. These stressed traditional doctrine based on historical sources and did not create an innovation, though the new formulas avoided the phrase "I absolve you." Some had argued from biblical testimony that it had to be retained: Jesus said, "Whose sins you forgive are forgiven" (John 20:23) and "Whatever you absolve on earth will be absolved in heaven" (Matt 18:18). But the group had other historical formulas showing that Christ absolves sins and does so by the ministry of the priest.[110]

The revisers foresaw difficulties when the words of absolution came into the vernacular languages. Even though the Constitution on the Sacred Liturgy said that Christ is present in all the sacraments (7), when the priest said "I absolve you," penitents—especially youth—might logically think that the priest and not Christ was absolving. The revisers therefore put into the appendix two formulas designed to make clear the forgiving ministry of Christ.[111]

The revisers noted that the phrase "I absolve you" is missing from all sources of the first millennium, appearing for the first time in the Roman-Germanic Pontifical around 950, and even there in a text of little importance. It appeared in a mid-twelfth-century homily of Radulfus Ardens, and then Thomas Aquinas favored its judicial character and considered it a central aspect. After that, the formula "I absolve you" was widely adopted. Nevertheless, the Constitution on the Sacred Liturgy had asked for consideration of all of history (23). The revisers wondered if the renewal of The Order of Penance could omit all the testimony of the entire first millennium.[112]

Furthermore, the revisers noted, the Eastern Rites had developed their own formulas, and only the Armenians, influenced by

---

110. Schemata n. 350, p. 2, citing the Vogel-Elze edition of the Roman-Germanic Pontifical, n. 246 and n. 249.

111. Schemata n. 350, p. 3.

112. Schemata n. 350, p. 4, citing homily LXIV by Radulfus on the major litanies (*Patrologia Latina* 155, 1900CD), delivered about the year 1150.

the West, used a phrase similar to "I absolve you." Instead, the Eastern Rites favored deprecative formulas, calling upon God to forgive through the intercession of the Church, or declarative formulas about the immediate activity of Christ who does forgive. New formulas after these models, then, would have ecumenical appeal.[113]

A month later, having reviewed the discussions thus far, including the question of providing more than one formula of absolution, the revisers proposed two additional alternative formulas that met their criteria. The first repeated the optative formula proposed in the previous two drafts:

> May our Lord Jesus Christ, who offered himself to the Father by sacrificing for us, and who conferred onto his Church the power of forgiving sins, himself absolve you by the grace of the Holy Spirit from your sins, and restore you into the perfect peace of the Church. Who lives and reigns.[114]

The next formula, declarative in structure, offered a slight variation from the second of the latest draft. It changed the word "redeemed" to "reconciled":

> Our Lord Jesus Christ, who by his passion and resurrection reconciled the world, forgives your sins through my ministry by the grace of the Holy Spirit and restores you into the full life of the Church. Who lives and reigns.[115]

The Congregation for Divine Worship had some difficulties with this plan. It noted that the Council's Constitution on the Sacred Liturgy asked for a more meaningful celebration of reconciliation, but it did not request multiple forms of abso-

---

113. Schemata n. 350, pp. 4–5.

114. Sacra Congregatio pro Cultu Divino, Schemata n. 356, De Pænitentia 11 (30 October 1969), p. 7.

115. Schemata n. 356, p. 7.

lution.[116] One solution was to let the conferences of bishops decide which of the possible forms of absolution to adopt, and whether more than one was acceptable.[117] Some feared that the deprecative or declarative formulas, by omitting the words "I absolve you" and using a prayer or statement of forgiveness, may fail to give the penitent certitude about being forgiven. Some suggested adding a few words about the Church's power to forgive.[118] Others felt that avoiding the phrase "I absolve you" does injustice to the biblical evidence from John 20:23 and Matthew 18:18.[119] When the Congregation revised its draft a few months later, summarizing all of its hard work, it kept these two alternative forms in an appendix.[120] It left the main form unchanged from the previous drafts:

> In the name of our Lord Jesus Christ and in the power
> of the Holy Spirit I absolve you from your sins and fully
> restore you into the peace of the Church.[121]

Another Congregation then took issue with the final wording and overruled some of the preferences of the Congregation for Divine Worship. On Wednesday, June 10, 1970, the Sacred Congregation for the Doctrine of the Faith decided that there had to be only one form of absolution. It then allowed episcopal conferences to propose different ones corresponding to the mentality of the people,[122] but no such formulas appeared in the published edition.

116. Schemata n. 356, p. 2.

117. Sacra Congregatio pro Cultu Divino, Schemata n. 356 bis, De Pænitentia 11 (30 October 1969), p. 3.

118. Schemata n. 356 bis, pp. 3–4.

119. Schemata n. 356 bis, p. 4.

120. Schemata n. 361, p. 53.

121. Schemata n. 361, p. 48.

122. Sacra Congregatio pro Cultu Divino, Schemata n. 387 addendum II (1 December 1972), p. 3.

In response, the Congregation for Divine Worship, apparently disappointed at the decision,[123] put effort into revising the singular formula within the body of the text. They addressed several concerns: It was not trinitarian. It did not refer to the paschal mystery. The terms expressing reconciliation with the Church were insufficiently clear, not distinguishing devotional confessions of lesser sins from those with grave sins that produced a rupture with the Church.[124]

The final two drafts came in October and November of 1972, over two years after the decision to use a single formula of absolution. In the first of these, for the words of absolution, the Congregation for Divine Worship retained the previous ritual's classic phrase, "I absolve you." It added a phrase about the paschal mystery, the effects of the death and resurrection of Christ. It mentions all three persons of the Trinity. To address the ecclesial dimension, the final phrase about restoring the penitent to the peace of the Church changed to a more direct expression about reconciling the penitent with the Church. This was more in keeping with the Constitution on the Church (11).[125] Reconciliation with the Church was simultaneous with reconciliation with God. "The mystery of the justification of the sinner with God is at the same time the mystery of the justification of the sinner with the Church."[126] The first of these final drafts crafted this formula:

> In the name of our Lord Jesus Christ, who reconciled
> the world to the Father by his passion and resurrection,

---

123. An undated, uncredited handwritten note on Schemata n. 279 bis, p. 10, held in the archives of the International Commission on English in the Liturgy, reads, "After much discussion and argumentation, they decided on this one instead of better formula in scheme, which some bishops claimed was not 'substantially same' as present formula!"

124. Schemata n. 387 addendum II, p. 3.

125. *Vatican II*, p. 15.

126. Schemata n. 387 addendum II, p. 4.

and in the power of the Holy Spirit I absolve you from
your sins, reconciling you fully with the Church.[127]

In the last of the drafts, two prepositions changed: "to
the Father" became "with the Father," and the prepositional
phrase "in the power" became an ablative form in Latin, probably best rendered as "by the power":

> In the name of our Lord Jesus Christ, who reconciled
> the world with the Father by his passion and resurrec-
> tion, and by the power of the Holy Spirit, I absolve you
> from your sins, reconciling you fully with the Church.[128]

In general the new formula met considerable approval for
its references to the Trinity, the paschal mystery, and reconciliation with the Church. Still, not everyone liked the results.
There were dozens of suggestions on how to mention the
Trinity and to express the relationship between forgiveness
and the paschal mystery. For example, Papali thought that
the translations would incorrectly emphasize one's horizontal
relationship to the community, rather than one's relationship
with God.[129] Pedro María Abellán of the Apostolic Penitentiary objected to the word "fully" because someone could
receive absolution in the internal forum.[130]

Balthasar Fischer objected on several grounds: the revision
removed the phrase "May our Lord Jesus Christ absolve you,"
which would have kept Christ at the center of the sacrament;
it removed the sign of the cross, which could still be given
even with an imposition of hands; and the last line presumed
that even those who committed venial sins were somehow
excluded from the Church. He proposed a different formula:

127. Schemata n. 386, pp. 22 and 33.
128. Schemata n. 387, pp. 28 and 34.
129. Schemata n. 387 addendum III, p. 1.
130. Schemata n. 387 addendum III, p. 24.

"May our Lord Jesus Christ absolve you by the power of the Holy Spirit, and by his authority I absolve you from your sins in the name of the Father ✚ and of the Son and of the Holy Spirit." Then he suggested that the confessor conclude in these or similar words: "Now may you again have full peace with God and with your brothers and sisters. May the Lord preserve this peace for you."[131]

The formula changed again for the published edition.[132] It mentions the roles of all three members of the Trinity: the Father of mercies, the reconciliation achieved by the Son's death and resurrection, and the gift of the Holy Spirit for the forgiveness of sins. The formula's opening declaration applies the paschal mystery to the forgiveness of sins. It makes an optative statement, expressing the desire that God the Father grant pardon and peace. It notes that God's pardon comes through the ministry of the Church, thus affirming the role of the priest, who represents the community through which reconciliation is happening. The formula concludes with an indicative statement that the priest absolves the penitent (OP 46). The priest gestures with one or both hands throughout the formula and then makes the sign of the cross as he pronounces the names of the Trinity, which return in the last line.

The biblical foundations for this forgiveness are Matthew 18:18 and John 20:23. In the first, the Vulgate uses the verb *solvo*, and in the second the verb *remitto*. In the formula, the word for the purpose of the Holy Spirit comes from the verb *remitto*, and the prayer is for God to grant *indulgentia*, or pardon. The priest, however, describes his action with the verb *absolvo*, a more direct connection to Matthew 18:18, where Jesus gave his followers the power to forgive. Thus, forgiveness comes from God, and the priest acts as the designated agent.

131. Schemata n. 387 addendum III, p. 25.
132. Bugnini, p. 674.

As in all the drafts, the penitent answers "Amen" to the words of absolution. This brief acclamation expresses one's faith and gratitude for forgiveness received.

Special Circumstances: Dispensation from Irregularity

Irregularities pertain to those who seek holy orders. The Code of Canon Law describes them in canon 1041. The list includes amentia, heresy, homicide, and attempted suicide. Dispensation from many irregularities is reserved to the Holy See. A bishop may dispense from others.

The Order of Penance includes a formula for such a dispensation. An authorized priest may use it either within or outside the sacrament of penance (Appendix I:3). If within the sacrament, it follows the bestowal of absolution.

The Proclamation of Praise of God and the Dismissal of the Penitent

The ceremony draws to its conclusion when the priest invites the penitent to give thanks to the Lord. The penitent answers, "For his mercy endures for ever" (OP 47). The dialogue expresses thankfulness that the penitent's sins have been forgiven, as it draws from the opening lines of Psalm 118 or 136, as suggested by one of the last drafts.[133] The priest dismisses the penitent in peace. In practice, though, not every priest initiates the dialogue; not every penitent has learned the response.

Other texts may substitute for this proclamation of God's praise and dismissal (OP 93). The first of these is the traditional closing to the fivefold absolution from the previous Roman Ritual. The only differences are the removal of the word "ever" from its description of the virginity of Mary and

133. Schemata n. 386, pp. 13 and 22.

the exchange of the word for "merits" with one for "intercession," as suggested in the late drafts.[134] No explanation is given for the first change, which surely does not intend to deny the perpetual virginity of Mary. The omission may represent the discovery of an earlier version of the formula or even a copy error. (All the schematas were written on typewriters.) This proclamation also adjoins the dismissal formula to go in peace.

The remaining options also suggest a conclusion. The second declares that the Lord has freed the penitent from sin and prays for the penitent's salvation. The priest proclaims glory to God, and the penitent answers, "Amen." Of these four options in OP 93, this is the only one that explicitly calls for the penitent's reply.

The third alludes to Psalm 32:2, a prayer that celebrates forgiveness. The priest invites the penitent to rejoice in the Lord and to go in peace.

The last option imitates the dismissal from Mass, inviting the penitent to go in peace and proclaim the works of God who saves.

The drafts had proposed similar formulas: "Your faith has saved you. Go in peace."[135] Or "Your sins are forgiven you: Go in peace." Or "Go in peace, and do not sin again." The revisers found the final formula in an uncited passage from the Cistercian Ritual. They proposed a penitent's response: "Thanks be to God," or "Glory to you, O Lord."[136]

The previous ceremony in the Roman Ritual had no dismissal of the penitent. The 1846 Ritual of Belley in France used, "Go in peace, and pray for me." However, the revisers wanted dismissals drawn from the gospels.[137] More suggestions came forward, including "May the Lord direct your heart in

134. Schemata n. 387, p. 48.
135. Schemata n. 386, pp. 13 and 22.
136. Schemata n. 251 allegatum II, p. 7.
137. Schemata n. 272, pp. 32–33.

the love of God and the patience of Christ" (2 Thess 3:5) or, inspired by 2 Maccabees 1:2, 4, "May God bless you, may he open your heart in his law and in his precepts, and may he give you peace."[138] These reappeared in a later draft.[139]

By implication, the penitent then leaves the presence of the priest. The rubric does not explicitly say so. This is surely an oversight, just as the rubric at the end of Mass instructs the priest to leave, but never tells the other ministers or the people to do so (Order of Mass 145). They all leave anyway.

One of the drafts addressed this oversight by including such a specific instruction. It does not appear in The Order of Penance, but it fittingly describes the conclusion of reconciling individuals:

> The penitent, rejoicing in having received the forgiveness of sins, continues his (her) conversion by a life of penitence in which is expressed the need for continual conversion, so that the Christian life may more and more be awash in the love of God, because "love covers a multitude of sins" (1 Pet 4:8).[140]

138. Schemata n. 279 bis, p. 3.
139. Schemata n. 387, p. 49.
140. Schemata n. 386, p. 13.

The Order for Reconciling
Several Penitents
with Individual Confession
and Absolution

Often called a "communal penance service," this order for reconciling several penitents possesses no direct precedent in the Roman Ritual for priests. Its antecedents lay rather in a bishop's reconciliation of those in the order of penitents, a ceremony found in the Roman Pontificals of the Middle Ages. The rite designed after the Second Vatican Council, however, focused on the communitarian nature of sin and forgiveness, whereas the historical precedents reconciled presumed sinful members of the community with presumed grace-filled members. In the twentieth-century ritual, all recognize their sin, and all seek forgiveness. In practice, even some confessors, moved by the meaning of the ceremony, confess their sins to another priest in attendance.

The ritual fulfilled a value expressed in the Constitution on the Sacred Liturgy (27): "It must be emphasized that rites which are meant to be celebrated in common, with the faithful present and actively participating, should as far as possible be celebrated in that way rather than by an individual and quasi-privately."[1] By its design, the first form of reconciliation is individual and private. The revisers sought a more communal alternative.

The group wondered if a single priest could offer the words of absolution once over an entire group of penitents, reconciling them simultaneously, as a bishop had done for the order of penitents in the Middle Ages. Some believed that a communal rite would help participants prepare to celebrate the individual rite, whereas others envisioned that parts of the ceremony could be conducted in common while individual confession and absolution followed.[2]

In the initial drafts, the group proposed the same format for individual confession. The ceremony began with the arrival of the penitent and the priest, the opening prayer, and the greeting. That much could be done in common. Then followed three parts still executed in private: the confession of sins, the dialogue with the confessor, and the imposition of the penance. The group envisioned that the remaining paragraphs could be done in common: the giving of absolution and the dismissal.[3] The revisers deliberately gave only a few details so that pastors had the greatest freedom in adapting the rite to local circumstances and persons.[4] Eventually the revisers enhanced the outline with music, emended texts, supplied multiple readings from Scripture including a gospel, and then added petitions and the Lord's Prayer.[5] At the time the ceremony carried the title "General Confession," signifying the communal acknowledgment of sin; however, some consultants thought that this would confuse those penitents who used the

---

1. *Vatican II*, p. 128.
2. Schemata n. 251 allegatum I, p. 1.
3. Schemata n. 265, pp. 2–3; Schemata n. 272, p. 34.
4. Schemata n. 265, p. 5.
5. Schemata n. 267, pp. 4–5.

same term to express their desire to summarize personal sins that they committed over some years.[6]

In the Middle Ages, the reconciliation of sinners spread over two events: communal entrance into the order of penitents and then, after a period of repentance, the communal ceremony of forgiveness. The first coincided with Ash Wednesday, and the second with Holy Thursday. In the sixth century, the Council of Agde and Caesarius of Arles testified that penitents received sackcloth from the bishop and abstained from communion during this time.[7] Their repentance was open, not private, and they interacted with the community as penitents.

The revisers knew of efforts to restore public penance in the twentieth century. Even the Constitution on the Sacred Liturgy reflected on the penitential elements of Lent that people carried out in common (109b):

> Further, as well as pointing out the social consequences of sin, the catechesis must impress on the minds of the faithful the distinctive character of penance as a detestation of sin because it is an offence against God. The role of the church in penitential practices is not to be omitted, and the need to pray for sinners should be emphasized.[8]

Thus the council knew about and promoted the communitarian dimensions of sin and forgiveness, especially as a characterization of Lent. Indeed, before the close of the Second Vatican Council, Dutch bishops had already formulated guidelines for communal celebrations, and the bishops of the council themselves participated in a "public penitential celebration" on September 14, 1965.[9]

6. Schemata n. 267, p. 6.
7. Schemata n. 272, p. 9.
8. *Vatican II*, p. 151.
9. Schemata n. 222, p. 7.

Some questioned whether one priest could give absolution over all who had confessed their sins to various priests. The group knew of historical examples of absolutions in the plural form, especially on Holy Thursday, when a bishop absolved groups of penitents together.[10] One proposal called for all the priests to offer the words of absolution together, each intending to absolve the people whose confessions he had heard. But the group found this inelegant and unnecessary. There were historical examples of penitents starting their period of repentance with a bishop and concluding it with a priest, having confessed to one cleric and been forgiven by another.[11] For these reasons, the group proposed that confession be individual, but absolution common.[12]

In the end, however, The Order of Penance has the confessor confer absolution on penitents one by one. This ensured the integrity of the sacrament. One late draft called it the Order for Reconciling Many Penitents at the Same Time with Individual Confession and Absolution,[13] then another removed the notion of simultaneity from the title, calling it the Order for Reconciling Many Penitents with Individual Confession and Absolution.[14] The communal nature of the experience became evident through hearing the Word of God, prayer, and the praise of God offered together after individuals had confessed and received their absolution.[15]

The Introductory Rites

The communal celebration opens with introductory rites: a song, a greeting, and a prayer. The ceremony begins when the

---

10. Schemata n. 272, p. 34.
11. Schemata n. 272, p. 35.
12. Schemata n. 361, pp. 31–32.
13. Schemata n. 386, p. 14.
14. Schemata n. 387, p. 29.
15. Schemata n. 386, p. 14.

faithful have assembled (OP 48), as does the Order of Mass. As noted above, the rubric that begins the reconciling of an individual penitent similarly notes the presence of one of the faithful, not just of the priest (OP 41). In the communal rite, the priest enters after the people have gathered.

For the song, the ritual book proposes two biblical verses. The first asks God to look upon the assembly in the abundance of his mercy. It comes from Psalm 69:17, which is also the entrance antiphon for Mass on the Saturday after Ash Wednesday. The second invites all to approach the throne of grace with boldness to receive mercy and grace. This comes from Hebrews 4:15 and is the entrance antiphon for Mass on Thursday of the Seventh Week of Easter. It appeared among many options in late drafts,[16] which first had proposed two other psalms: The refrain, "O Lord our God, you are patient and possessing great mercy," would accompany Psalm 86, especially verses 1-6, 11-12, and 15. Or all could sing the refrain, "As a Father has mercy on his children, so does the Lord show mercy to those who fear him," with Psalm 103, especially verses 1-5, 8-14, 15-18.[17] Other options were Psalm 24:1-6; Psalm 95:1-11; Psalm 145:3-4, 8-9, 14-15, 17-18, 19-20; and Psalm 146:2-10. The published book allows other liturgical songs (OP 48), so a musician could choose one of these earlier suggestions.

The priest greets the people with one of several proposed formulas (OP 49). The first is based on 1 Timothy 1:2 and Titus 1:4 and wishes the grace, mercy, and peace that comes from God the Father and from Christ. The second alludes to Revelation 1:4-6, which says that Christ freed the faithful from their sins by his own blood. Both these greetings appeared in late drafts.[18]

---

16. Schemata n. 386, p. 23; Schemata n. 387, p. 41.
17. Schemata n. 386, p. 23; Schemata n. 387, p. 29.
18. Schemata n. 386, p. 23; and Schemata n. 387, p. 29.

Other options include a greeting from 2 John 3, wishing grace and peace from the Father and the Son, in this case in truth and in love (OP 94). Another cites 2 Maccabees 1:4-5, inviting the faithful to open their hearts to God's law to receive peace and reconciliation (OP 95). The last comes from Galatians 1:3-5, which declares that Christ gave himself up for our sins (OP 96). These few selections remain from a longer list of options in the draft.[19] Alternatively, the priest may choose any greeting from the Order of Mass (OP 96).

The priest or another minister then instructs the faithful on the importance of the service (OP 49). The other minister could be a deacon or a catechist, for example.

The priest invites all to pray for the grace of true and fruitful repentance (OP 50). In one draft, the deacon invited all to kneel or bow their heads for a time of silence before standing erect again for prayer.[20] The published book removed that instruction, possibly to align the people's posture with the one they typically assume for a presidential prayer at Mass. However, the change in posture does appear a few paragraphs later in the general confession of sins (OP 54). As will be seen later in the book, a change in posture does happen at the prayer that opens a penitential celebration during Lent (OP 9, Appendix II, 9 and 15).

The priest selects a prayer from several options. In the first he asks God for pardon and peace to the sinner. The same prayer serves as the collect for the Mass for the Forgiveness of Sins in the Missal. It comes from a collection of penitential prayers in the ninth-century Gregorian Sacramentary.[21] The second option comes from a Visigoth prayer book of the

19. Schemata n. 387, pp. 50–51.
20. Schemata n. 386, p. 24.
21. Schemata n. 387, p. 30, citing *Le sacramentaire grégorien: Ses principales formes d'après les plus anciens manuscrits*, ed. Jean Deshusses, vol. 1, Spicilegium Friburgense (Fribourg: Éditions universitaires, 1979), n. 842, among its prayers offered because of sins.

Mozarabic tradition[22] and asks for the gift of the Holy Spirit to wash the sinners in repentance and make them a living sacrifice, an allusion to Romans 12:1 (OP 50).

Another option, from the same collection of penitential prayers in the Gregorian Sacramentary,[23] asks for absolution that all may serve the Lord in freedom of heart, an allusion to Galatians 5:13 (OP 97). The next alludes to the account of God's response to Moses' prayer after the people worshiped a golden calf (Exod 32:14) and is based on a prayer from the eighth-century Gelasian Sacramentary,[24] offered over public penitents at the beginning of Lent (OP 98).

The next prays for open eyes to see personal wrong, the unity of what sin has divided, healing for those wounded, and new life to those held captive (OP 99). It relies on several biblical passages: Hebrews 4:16, which invites the faithful to approach the throne of grace for timely help; 2 Corinthians 4:14-18, on the promise of resurrection; and John 17:3, from Jesus' prayer at the Last Supper that his followers may know the only God and the one he sent. It also draws from part of the sequence for Pentecost, the *Veni Creator*, where it prays for healing. The source of this complex prayer is uncredited,[25] so one of the revisers may have composed it.

The last option prays that God, who loves conversion, will help his people return and live, confess their sins, give thanks for forgiveness, and do the truth in charity (OP 100). It relies on Ezekiel 18:23, 32; and 33:11, 18, which say that God wills not the death of a sinner; and Ephesians 4:15, which assures spiritual growth for those who live or speak the truth in charity. It too is uncredited in the draft[26] and has only a minor variation in the published form, so it too may be an original

---

22. Schemata n. 386, p. 24; Schemata n. 387, p. 30.
23. Schemata n. 387, p. 51, citing n. 846.
24. Schemata n. 387, p. 52, citing n. 81.
25. Schemata n. 387, p. 52.
26. Schemata n. 387, p. 53.

work for The Order of Penance. The draft offered other options that the published edition did not adopt.

The Celebration of the Word of God

The people listen to the Word of God before they confess their sins. This communal hearing underscores shared sinfulness and shared repentance among the gathered assembly, who seek forgiveness and new direction from God. It also answers one of the expectations of the Constitution on the Sacred Liturgy, that the Word of God be part of liturgical celebrations (24).

The order presents a myriad of options, proposing two complete sets of readings imitating the structure of the Liturgy of the Word on Sundays through most of the liturgical year: a first reading from the Old Testament, a responsorial psalm, a reading from the New Testament, an acclamation, and a passage from the gospels. These two models explore the themes of love as the fullness of the law and the renewal of one's mind, respectively (OP 51). Both appeared in the late drafts with minor variations.[27] There, the first model carried only one gospel selection, Matthew 22:34-40. The alternative in OP 51 (John 13:34-35, 15:10-13) was the gospel for the second model in the draft. The published edition moved it to its present position. For the second model, it replaced both this passage and its verse before the gospel (John 15:11) with Matthew 5:1-12 and Matthew 11:28.

One draft proposed a responsory after the second reading, such as one finds in the Office of Readings in the Liturgy of the Hours, instead of a gospel acclamation. The one for the first model was based on Colossians 1:12-14 and 1 John 4:10. The second model drew from Romans 5:8, 20, and then from Romans 5:11.[28]

27. Schemata n. 386, p. 25; Schemata n. 387, p. 31.
28. Schemata n. 386, p. 25.

The collection of various texts in the fourth chapter offers a staggering 101 other options for planners to peruse (OP 101–201), some of which are quite lengthy. These readings actually shorten the list of 118 passages from one of the drafts.[29] The selection aimed to emphasize several themes: the voice of God calling people to conversion and ever greater conformity to Christ; revealing the mystery of reconciliation through the death and resurrection of Christ and through the gift of the Holy Spirit; and the judgment of God concerning good and evil in human life, given to enlighten and scrutinize one's conscience.[30]

A homily follows the readings, reflects on them, and helps penitents examine their consciences and renew their lives (OP 52). All these points come from the drafts and illustrate the purpose of the sacrament.[31] Moved by the Word of God, contrite penitents seek forgiveness for the past and a new start to a more faithful future.

The drafts added other points: The homily should lead penitents to detest their sins that rejected the love and grace of God—sins committed against themselves, the Church, and all others.[32] The homily should help the faithful recall their sins committed against God, but also against the community, their neighbor, and themselves. To this end, the people were to recall the infinite mercy of God, which is greater than human iniquities; the necessary interior repentance by which people are sincerely disposed to repair the damages of sin; the social nature of grace and sin, in which all are one in executing good or ill as they act as members of one body; and the need of one's own reparation, which derives power from the reparation of Christ, and which demands above all, besides works of repentance, the exercise of true charity toward God and neighbor.[33]

29. Schemata n. 361, pp. 55–57.
30. Schemata n. 386, p. 17; Schemata n. 387, p. 17.
31. Schemata n. 387, p. 31.
32. Schemata n. 386, p. 25.
33. Schemata n. 386, p. 17; Schemata n. 387, p. 17.

An examination of conscience follows this homily. This may take place in silence as all reflect on the admonitions received. Or the priest, deacon, or another minister may lead a kind of litany of sins, to help people prepare to confess (OP 53). The description comes directly from the drafts.[34]

The drafts allowed the litany to replace the homily, as long as it referenced the Scriptures that all heard. Such a litany would facilitate an examination of conscience and stir up contrition.[35] Permission to substitute the homily with a litany remains (OP 26).

The Rite of Reconciliation

The next parts of the ceremony feel familiar to those with experience of individual confession and absolution. All make a general confession of sins. The deacon or another minister invites all to kneel or bow. All recite a general formula, such as the *Confiteor* from the Order of Mass. They stand and may recite a litany or sing an appropriate liturgical song. The Lord's Prayer always concludes this general confession, an immediate preparation for each individual's confession of particular sins (OP 54). These instructions come from the late drafts.[36]

Invitation to the General Confession of Sins

The ritual book offers several examples. To begin, a deacon or another minister invites the community to begin the general confession. Perhaps the presider does not make this invitation because he is the confessor, and this section of the ritual prepares those who will confess to him. The first two examples (OP 54) come from the drafts.[37]

---

34. Schemata n. 386, p. 25; Schemata n. 387, p. 32.
35. Schemata n. 386, p. 18; Schemata n. 387, p. 17.
36. Schemata n. 386, p. 18; Schemata n. 387, p. 18.
37. Schemata n. 386, pp. 25–27; Schemata n. 387, pp. 32–33.

In the first example the minister asks all to confess their sins and pray that all may be saved. The invitation alludes to James 5:16, which makes the same appeal (OP 54).

In the second example the minister asks all to recall the kindness of God, confess their sins, and obtain mercy. The words allude to Titus 3:4, which proclaims the kindness and generous love of God, which appeared in Jesus Christ (OP 54).

Later, the book supplies alternative invitations to the general confession (OP 202). Several of these address the Father. The first recalls that God desires not the death of sinners but that they turn back and live, a reference to Ezekiel 18:23, 32; and 33:11, 18. The minister invites the people's earnest plea lest they return to regrettable actions in the future. The response begs the Lord to spare his people (OP 202.1). This invitation appeared in the draft,[38] which drew the words from the Gelasian Sacramentary, where they were used to introduce a prayer for assigning penance.

The next invites confident prayer to God who possesses a multitude of mercies and pardons those who repent, that he may hear those who confess (OP 202.2). The draft drew this from the Rheinau Sacramentary.[39]

The next recalls that God handed over Jesus for our transgressions and raised him for our justification, a reference to Romans 4:25 (OP 202.3). The draft drew this from the introduction to the invocations at Friday Evening Prayer in the third week of the cycle for Ordinary Time in the revised Liturgy of the Hours.[40]

The fourth example recalls the image of the father of the prodigal son (Luke 15:20). God, too, awaits the return of his children and embraces them when they repent. One response recalls the same parable, echoing the line that the prodigal son

---

38. Schemata n. 387, p. 60, citing 1702–3 in the Gelasian Sacramentary.
39. Schemata n. 387, p. 60, citing Rheinau Sacramentary 30, n. 1327.
40. Schemata n. 387, p. 60.

rehearsed when he felt no longer deserving to be called his father's child (OP 202.4). The introduction and the responses came from the draft.[41]

The last example brings to the fore the image of God in Ezekiel 34:16, a shepherd who seeks out and brings back the lost, and who strengthens the weak. The people's response prays for the healing of spiritual infirmities (OP 202.5). Both the introduction and the responses came from the draft.[42]

In other examples, the introduction invites prayer to Jesus Christ (OP 203). The first recalls his victory over sin and death and seeks pardon from God, but also reconciliation with the Church. This appeared in the draft, which cites numbers 11 and 59 of the Council's Dogmatic Constitution on the Church, *Lumen Gentium*, as the source.[43]

The second example draws a line from Eucharistic Prayer II, recalling that Christ willingly entered his passion and death for the salvation of all. People may therefore approach him with confidence (OP 203.2). The draft cites number 4 of the Council's Declaration on the Relation of the Church to Non-Christian Religions, *Nostra Aetate*, as the source.[44] "Christ out of infinite love freely underwent suffering and death because of the sins of all, so that all might attain salvation (4)."[45]

The third example calls Christ the Good Shepherd who carries back the lost sheep with rejoicing, alluding to Matthew 18:10-14; Luke 15:1-7; and John 10:3-4. The people ask Christ to seek them out and carry them home (OP 203.3). This introduction and the people's response came from the draft, which specifically cited Luke 15:4-7.[46]

41. Schemata n. 387, p. 60.
42. Schemata n. 387, p. 60.
43. Schemata n. 387, p. 61.
44. Schemata n. 387, p. 61.
45. *Vatican II*, p. 574.
46. Schemata n. 387, p. 61.

The fourth invites prayers to Christ who bore the sins of humanity on the tree of the cross and healed their wounds, alluding to 1 Peter 2:24 and Romans 6:11. In one response, the people repeat the words of Peter in John's gospel, affirming that there is nowhere else to turn: Christ, the Son of God, has the words of eternal life. The second pleads for mercy (OP 203.4). The invitation and the responses both come from the draft, which cites John 6:68-69 for the first response and Mark 9:22 for the second, where the father of a boy possessed by a mute spirit appeals to Jesus to help—if he can.[47]

The final example recalls that Christ was handed over for the sins of humanity and rose for its justification, alluding to Romans 4:25. The people's response acclaims Christ as Savior or appeals to the Son of the living God for mercy, citing Peter's confession of faith (Matt 16:16). In several of these introductions, people may take comfort in remembering Peter, whose denial of Jesus made him one of the gospel's most public grave sinners, and who nonetheless experienced forgiveness (OP 203.5). The introduction and two responses come from the draft.[48]

Litany

After the *Confiteor* in the first example, the minister introduces and leads a litany of repentance. These petitions trace a desirable sequence of events: the repentance of sinners, the pardon of God, the restoration of the sinner's holiness and splendor of baptism; and then the sinner's return to participation at the altar, faithfulness to sacraments, witness in the world, and everlasting life (OP 54). The list is based on one from the drafts.[49]

47. Schemata n. 387, p. 61.
48. Schemata n. 387, p. 61.
49. Schemata n. 267, p. 8; Schemata n. 386, p. 26; Schemata n. 387, pp. 32–33.

After the *Confiteor* in the second example, the minister leads a different litany (OP 54). This one is addressed to Christ, the righteous advocate with the Father. It alludes to 1 John 2:1, which calls Jesus Christ the righteous one, a sinner's advocate with the Father. The litany surveys the biography of Jesus through the lens of forgiveness: he came to bring good news to the poor (Luke 4:18) and to call sinners, not the righteous (Matt 9:13; Mark 2:17; Luke 5:32); he forgave the woman who loved much (Luke 7:47) and ate with tax collectors and sinners (Luke 5:30); he embodied the parable's shepherd, who carried the lost sheep on his shoulders (Luke 15:5); he did not condemn the woman caught in adultery (John 8:11); he called Zacchaeus to conversion (Luke 19:5-10) and promised paradise to the repentant thief (Luke 23:43); and he sits at the right hand of the Father to intercede for sinners (Rom 8:34). This second example is similarly a lightly edited version of one from the drafts.[50]

More examples appear later in the book. A rubric there indicates that one intercession should always be for true conversion of heart, highlighting one purpose of the renewed celebration: putting intentionality into the ritual. The first set offers a series of invocations to the Father (OP 204.1). The first of these outlines a spiritual journey of repentance, asking the Father for complete remission and a restoration of full communion, admission to the sacrament of reconciliation, conversion of heart, and rescue from slavery to sin. More intentions pray for the fruits of reconciliation, such as becoming a living sign of God's love, accepting and pursuing peace, learning love and forgiveness, a worthy participation in the Eucharist, and preparation for the life to come. Several of these refer to scriptural passages: being set free from slavery to sin and being led to freedom (Rom 8:21); receiving a wedding

50. Schemata n. 267, p. 8; Schemata n. 386, p. 27; Schemata n. 387, pp. 33–34.

garment for feasting at the Lord's table (Matt 22:11); hoping God will not in anger reprove the sinner (Pss 6:2, 38:2); and stripping off old ways and becoming capable of new ways of holiness (Col 3:9). The entire list is drawn from the draft.[51]

The second set addressed to the Father offers the option of a variable response to each invocation (OP 204.2). These pray for forgiveness of individual sin and the restoration of unity in God's family, a purification of the Church, and the return of others guilty of sin and scandal. The series continues with allusions to scriptural passages: carrying the death of the Son, whose Body has brought life (2 Cor 4:10); admitting the greatness of one's sins (1 Chr 21:8); being received with humble spirit and contrite heart (Dan 3:39); repenting of wickedness and evil (Dan 9:5); and praying that sins will be cast into the depths of the sea (Mic 7:19).

The first ten of these invocations copy petitions near the end of Morning and Evening Prayer in the Liturgy of the Hours. The remainder are based on biblical passages:[52]

1. First week of Lent, Monday Morning Prayer, last petition

2. First week of Lent, Tuesday Morning Prayer, last petition

3. First week of Lent, Wednesday Evening Prayer, fourth petition

4. First week of Lent, Thursday Morning Prayer, last petition

5. Second week of Lent, Tuesday Morning Prayer, last petition, though without the reference to the saving days of Lent

6. Second week of Lent, Tuesday Evening Prayer, fourth petition

51. Schemata n. 387, p. 62.
52. Schemata n. 387, p. 63.

7. Second week of Lent, Wednesday Morning Prayer, last petition

8. Third week of Ordinary Time, Friday Evening Prayer, first petition

9. Third week of Ordinary Time, Friday Evening Prayer, third petition

10. Fourth week of Ordinary Time, Friday Morning Prayer, third petition

11. Daniel 3:29-30

12. Micah 7:19

13. Psalm 32:11

The second series contains invocations to Christ. The first set turns more than thirty biblical passages into appeals to Christ (OP 205.1). The ritual book meticulously cites each verse. They all come from the New Testament and appear in biblical order until the last group referring to the gospels. These depict a biography of Jesus: coming into the world to seek what was lost (Matt 18:11), his ministry to forgive sins (Mark 2:10), sharing that ministry with the apostles (Matt 16:19 and 18:18), laying down his life for his sheep (John 10:11), and showing the way to the Father (John 14:6). The complete list of invocations appeared in the draft.[53]

The second set addressed to Christ offers the option of a variable response to each invocation (OP 205.2). These pray for healing of wounds, newness of heart, acceptance of penance, and the intercession of Mary. Biblical references include the physician of sinners (Matt 9:12; Mark 2:17; Luke 5:31), stripping off one's old self (Col 3:9), the forgiveness of the penitent woman (Luke 7:47), the found sheep on the shoul-

---

53. Schemata n. 387, pp. 64–65.

ders of the shepherd (Luke 15:5), and the promise of paradise to the thief (Luke 23:43).

Many of these also come from the Liturgy of the Hours:

1. First week of Lent, Sunday Morning Prayer, last petition

2. Second week of Lent, Sunday first Vespers, third petition

3. Friday after Ash Wednesday, Evening Prayer, first petition, with a slight variation

4. Saturday after Ash Wednesday, Morning Prayer, last petition

5. Fourth week of Ordinary Time, Friday Evening Prayer, fourth petition, first half

6. Fourth week of Ordinary Time, Friday Evening Prayer, fourth petition, second half

7. No source is given, but its reference to the good thief resembles his inclusion in a similar list (OP 54, second example).

8. No source is given, but it seems to refer to the promise of resurrection in Romans 6:5.[54]

The Lord's Prayer follows, and the priest concludes the general confession with a prayer. In the first example, he asks that the people be set free from sin and render thanks to God (OP 54). In the second example, he introduces the Lord's Prayer, reminding people of the importance of mutual forgiveness. The drafts had also included the Lord's Prayer, even insisting upon it.[55] Then the priest prays that the help the people

54. Schemata n. 387, p. 65.
55. Schemata n. 265, p. 7; Schemata n. 267, p. 5.

receive may lead to a holy way of life. This is also the collect from Friday of the Fourth Week of Lent.

Individual Confession and Absolution

The priests occupy "suitable locations" (OP 55). In practice, these are often spread throughout a church, distant enough from one another for confessions to remain private. If the priest who presides is wearing a microphone, he shuts it off. One or more priests may take up a position inside confessionals where people present themselves anonymously. Otherwise, in practice, many of the penitents confess face-to-face to a priest who does or does not know them, as the penitent prefers. The two may take whatever posture seems appropriate. Often the two are standing, which seems to focus the conversation.

The use of confessionals may cause the practical difficulty that penitents presume from entering the space that they are to conduct their confession as usual: starting with the sign of the cross and a formula of general confession before confessing their sins, reciting an act of contrition, and finishing the concluding dialogue with the priest. However, those elements are executed in common. Penitents accustomed to beginning and ending a confession without those elements may not fully appreciate the distinction between an individual confession and the communal celebration.

Penitents approach the priest of their choice, confess their sins, accept a penance and receive absolution. Each penitent answers, "Amen."

As mentioned above, throughout the early drafts, the revisers envisioned that the presider would absolve the entire group at once. This would have accented the communal nature of sin and forgiveness. Sufficient historical examples seemed to pave the way, but the Vatican kept individual absolution with each confession. This altered the design of the celebration and lengthened its time, but it reassured each penitent that their sins were heard and forgiven.

Each priest recites the same words of absolution and uses the same gesture. He either extends hands over the head of the penitent or raises his right hand.

When a late draft finally accepted this procedure, it seemed mindful that the time for individual confession would lengthen. It offered suggestions to help pass the time: a penitential song expressing the mercy of God, the reading of a psalm or a gospel, or the playing of the organ or other instruments.[56] Some have noted with dissatisfaction that what people experience at a communal penance service is a communal waiting service, handling the extra minutes in restlessness while others confess their sins. The challenge intensifies when children outnumber other participants. The revisers had not faced this practical difficulty partly because they envisioned that absolution would take place in common.

Proclamation of Praise for God's Mercy

Newly forgiven, the participants praise God for the gift of mercy (OP 56). The priest invites the people to give thanks. He encourages them to lead a life of goodness so that others may come to know the grace of repentance. This last element addresses the concern that the sacrament meaningfully take root in the forgiven person's life.

All sing a psalm or a hymn, or they offer a litany of thanksgiving for God's power (OP 56). Suggestions include the *Magnificat* (Luke 1:46-55), or select verses from Psalm 136, as recommended in the same draft that also proposed Psalm 118:1-9, 13-19, and 28-29.[57] Later the book suggests over a dozen other options (OP 206). Most of these come from the book of Psalms, though the Old Testament prophets and New Testament canticles also contribute to the list. Through such

56. Schemata n. 387, p. 18.
57. Schemata n. 387, p. 35.

verses the community uses the Word of God to give thanks to God. All these options appeared in the draft.[58]

Although the rubric suggests a litany, it gives no examples apart from the recommended verses of Psalm 136, which themselves form a litany of praise for the wonders that God has done. A local community could develop its own litany, listing reasons for thanking God at this time.

The title for this section is how the drafts entitled the conversation at the beginning of an individual confession, as noted above in OP 43. The priest or the penitent read a brief line from the Scriptures that proclaimed God's mercy. In that position, this same title gave assurance for what God was about to do. The title moved here to offer thanksgiving for what God has done.

Concluding Prayer of Thanksgiving

The priest offers a final prayer of thanksgiving to God (OP 57). The first option praises God, who created and restored human nature (an allusion to the Christmas collect in the Roman Missal's Mass during the Day), who pursues sinners with a father's love, who sent his Son to destroy sin, who poured the Holy Spirit into the hearts of his children (alluding to Romans 5:5), and who sent the sacraments to transform his people more fully into the image of Christ. For all of this, the priest leads the community in expressing its "Amen" of thanksgiving. This prayer appeared uncredited in the draft,[59] so one of the revisers may have composed it.

The second option in OP 57 is a briefer prayer asking that those who have received the Father's mercy may become a sign of his love in the world. It addresses the concern that confession and penance bear fruit in the life of the penitent.

58. Schemata n. 387, pp. 66–67.
59. Schemata n. 387, p. 35.

It also appeared uncredited among a longer list of options in the draft.[60]

Another option for this prayer opens redolent of a preface at Mass, declaring that it is right and just always and everywhere to give thanks to God. Then, more soberly, it stresses both the chastisement God gives in correcting those who waver from the divine law and the pardon God mercifully gives to spare people from eternal punishment (OP 207). The draft gathered this prayer from the early eighth-century Gothic Missal, where it served as a preface for Mass during Lent.[61]

The next option recalls how God so loved the world that he sent his Son for salvation (John 3:16) and the role of the Son's passion and resurrection in redeeming the family of the faithful, while praying for God's continuing presence. Looking ahead to the fruits of penitence, the prayer asks for fear of God, faith, justice, devotion, truthfulness, and discipline that lead to immortal rewards (OP 208). The draft abbreviated this from another prayer in the Gothic Missal, part of a collect for a Mass at the close of the Easter octave.[62]

Yet another alternative for this prayer addresses Christ, who gave an example of humility and patient suffering (alluding to Phil 2:5-7), and asks for perseverance in holding what is good. It faces the reality that people sin, but prays that they be raised up in repentance (OP 209). The Gothic Missal placed this collect as the third among its six sets of Mass texts for use on Sundays.[63]

The next recalls Romans 5:8-9 when it praises God who makes sinners just (OP 210). It asks for the courage of perseverance in the works of those justified by faith (Rom 5:1). It comes from the eighth-century Old Gallic Missal.[64]

60. Schemata n. 387, p. 68.
61. Schemata n. 387, p. 67, citing the Gothic Missal n. 195.
62. Schemata n. 387, p. 67, citing the Gothic Missal n. 313.
63. Schemata n. 387, p. 67, citing the Gothic Missal n. 500.
64. Schemata n. 387, p. 68, citing the Old Gallic Missal n. 251.

The last option recalls the Lord's Prayer (Matt 6:9-13; Luke 11:2-4). It calls God "our Father" who forgives, and it prays for the grace of mutual forgiveness among those who strive to achieve peace in the world (OP 211). It is uncredited in the draft, so one of the revisers probably composed it.[65]

The Concluding Rites

The ceremony concludes with a blessing from the priest and a dismissal from the deacon. In the blessing, the priest prays that the Lord guide people in love and patience (2 Thess 3:5), that they walk in newness of life (Rom 6:4), and that they ever please God (OP 58). The entire blessing came from a draft,[66] and the first element reappeared by itself as another option in a subsequent draft.[67]

Another formula prays for the blessing of each Person of the Trinity (OP 212). It comes directly from an option in the Order of Mass (Blessings at the End of Mass and Prayers over the People).

Another prays more elaborately for the blessing of the Father, who gives birth to eternal life; the salvation coming from the Son, who died and rose; and sanctification from the Spirit, who leads those forgiven back on the right path (OP 213). This blessing recalls that the Spirit has been poured into the hearts of the faithful (Rom 5:5).

The final option is also trinitarian (OP 214). It prays for the blessing of the Father, who has adopted the faithful as his children (Rom 8:15; Gal 4:5). It pleads for the aid of the Son, who receives the faithful as his brothers and sisters. It asks for the presence of the Spirit, who makes the faithful his temple (1 Cor 6:19). These final three options are from the last draft.[68]

65. Schemata n. 387, p. 68.
66. Schemata n. 387, p. 36.
67. Schemata n. 387, p. 49.
68. Schemata n. 387, p. 69.

The deacon has only one recommended formula for dismissal, proclaiming that the Lord has forgiven the people their sins (OP 59), as in the last draft.[69] This imitates a common conclusion of the Mass. The deacon has the freedom to use some other appropriate formula. In the absence of a deacon, another minister—even one non-ordained—or the priest may dismiss the assembly.

The communal penance service has been often used in parishes during Advent and Lent to help large numbers of people prepare for Christmas and Easter. However, nothing in the ceremony limits it to those times of year. Those are times when many Catholics seek the sacrament of reconciliation, in order to celebrate the holiest days of the liturgical year with a clean heart and new spirit.

Priests generously give their time during these busy seasons to make themselves available for confession. Some priests use the occasion for socializing among themselves before or after the service because they gather infrequently to enjoy one another's company and share the joys and challenges of their ministry.

The service has its strengths and weaknesses. It reinforces the communal nature of sin and forgiveness, one of the goals of the revision. However, in some respects the ceremony looks better on paper than in act. Many of the faithful, who are accustomed to spending only a few minutes confessing their sins, tire of the lengthy ceremony and depart the service immediately after receiving their own absolution, rather than wait for the concluding acts of thanksgiving and dismissal. Many come more for personal forgiveness than communal celebration. Indeed, sometimes the confessing of sins can take over an hour, and the faithful may succumb anew to the sin of impatience while others confess. In many parishes, offering more hours for individual confessions serves the people better than a communal penance service.

---

69. Schemata n. 387, p. 36.

5

The Order for Reconciling Several Penitents with General Confession and Absolution

Circumstances Today

The Order of Penance reminds the faithful that individual confession and absolution are the only ordinary means by which they progress from the depths of grave sin toward reconciliation with God and the Church (OP 31). Those twin purposes of reconciliation strengthen the case for the sacrament. The priest aids both purposes, for God has entrusted him with this ministry, and he represents the community of the faithful with whom reconciliation is also achieved.

Nonetheless, in some cases the usual form of confessing sins is impossible. The Order of Penance offers two scenarios: One is when death is imminent, the number of the faithful is large, and the time is insufficient for a priest to hear individual confessions. The other condition does not concern the threat of death, but a chronic situation in which the penitents so outnumber the confessors available within a limited period of time that they would be unduly deprived of the grace of the sacrament and of holy communion through no fault of their own.

An example of the first scenario happened in Hawaii in early 2018, when a false missile alert lit up cell phones throughout the islands. Assuming that the threat was real, as it claimed to be, the bishop appropriately offered general absolution to a group of the faithful.[1] In 2020 at the height of the COVID-19 pandemic, when physical proximity between humans threatened illness and death, the Vatican's Apostolic Penitentiary permitted a broader use of general absolution.[2]

An example of the second scenario is mission lands where priests rarely visit some parts of the Catholic population. When their visit permits time for Mass, but not much more, they may administer general absolution so that the faithful may receive communion. All hope that the next visit of a priest affords more time for confessions.

In 1988, the United States Conference of Catholic Bishops agreed to a complementary norm for canon 961 §1, 2°, which universally permits authorizing general absolution if confessors are unavailable "for a long while."[3] The local norm considers the length of time required for such an absence to constitute a grave necessity would be one month.[4] Archbishop Francis

1. Ben Gutierrez, "Fearing Inbound Missile, Honolulu's Bishop Gave Rite of Absolution to Those at Mass," *Hawaii News Now*, updated 20 January 2018, https://www.hawaiinewsnow.com/story/37309262/catholic -bishop-performs-rare-rite-during-false-missile-alert/.

2. "Note from the Apostolic Penitentiary on the Sacrament of Reconciliation in the Current Pandemic," Holy See Press Office, 20 March 2020, https://press.vatican.va/content/salastampa/en/bollettino/pubblico /2020/03/20/200320d.html.

3. https://www.vatican.va/archive/cod-iuris-canonici/eng/documents /cic_lib4-cann959-997_en.html.

4. United States Conference of Catholic Bishops, Canonical Affairs & Church Governance, Complementary Norms, canon 961 §1, 2°, https://www.usccb.org/committees/canonical-affairs-church-governance /complementary-norms#tab--canon-961-§1-2°-general-absolution.

T. Hurley had already asserted that the conditions for general absolution existed in the State of Alaska, "where traveling by plane to go to confession would be too expensive for a venial sin and too dangerous for a mortal sin."[5]

In the past, some bishops approved the use of this form even for occasions such as parish penance services in Advent and Lent, when the number of penitents was large, and the number of confessors was few. One American archbishop came under Vatican investigation for frequently granting priests permission to use general absolution.[6] Church law envisions a more suddenly urgent or perpetually chronic situation.

Circumstances in History

Some of those preparing the revised ritual favored more broad usage and appealed to pastoral considerations. They argued that sometimes the number of penitents so exceeds the number of priests that there is no time to hear all the sins "with the tranquility and dignity that befits the sacrament." In mission lands the priest may visit an area rarely, and hearing individual confessions would take time away from the most serious of needs, such as "the instruction of catechumens and of the faithful, visiting the sick, preaching the gospel, and preparing couples for matrimony." Some confessions may happen so quickly that absolution seems mechanical without sufficient exhortation or the possibility of true dialogue.[7]

The revisers collected a dossier of the Roman Curia's previous permissions. For example, during World War I, when the mobilizing of soldiers and the danger of death allowed

5. Lydia Chavez, "Reporter's Notebook: A Red Letter for a 'Martyr,'" *New York Times*, 13 November 1986.

6. Greg Magnoni, "Standing-Room-Only Crowd Honors Life of Archbishop Emeritus Raymond G. Hunthausen," *Northwest Catholic*, 1 August 2018, https://nwcatholic.org/news/greg-magnoni/standing-room-only -crowd-honors-life-of-archbishop-emeritus-raymond-g-hunthausen.

7. Schemata n. 272, p. 38.

no time for individual confessions, priests could offer general absolution. The Vatican authorized the same during World War II, when soldiers in captivity had no opportunity for private confession.[8] In those circumstances, the Apostolic Penitentiary urged sinners at least to show some outward sign of repentance, if possible, such as striking the chest.[9]

In 1962 and 1963, amid dangers that some of the faithful would suffer persecution, the Congregation on the Propagation of the Faith allowed priests to absolve groups of sinners by a "most special faculty."[10] In 1966 the same congregation permitted some priests in Nairobi, Kenya, to give general absolution "at the vigils of the great religious solemnities," probably Christmas and Easter, "when the number of the faithful who wish to confess their sins becomes excessive," but required those in grave sin to confess individually to priests when it became possible.[11]

The Ritual

The structure of this ceremony imitates the one for a communal celebration with individual confession and absolution. If there is no time for such a liturgy, the priest uses the short form: a reading from Scripture if appropriate, the instruction explaining proper procedures, the proposal of an act of satisfaction, the penitents' general confession, and absolution (OP 64). If there is no time even for that, he may give the abbreviated formula of absolution, using only the essential words (OP 65).

Whenever the full ritual may take place, it opens the same way as a communal celebration in the previous chapter. After

---

8. Schemata n. 272, p. 39; Schemata n. 318, p. 10.
9. Schemata n. 272, p. 40.
10. Schemata n. 272, p. 42.
11. Schemata n. 272, p. 41; Schemata n. 318, p. 10.

the homily, those who seek absolution repent silently, resolve to refrain from these sins again, intend to repair harms, promise to confess individual grave sins that cannot be confessed aloud in this moment, and accept or even add to the act of satisfaction that the priest gives (OP 60).

A deacon or another minister invites all to kneel or bow down to mark their repentance (OP 61). This change in posture, evident also in the drafts,[12] replaces the usual physical proximity between the penitent and the confessor. The penitents make a general act of contrition together and add the Lord's Prayer.

The words of absolution may take a different form (OP 62). First the priest implores the assistance of each Person of the Holy Trinity. He recalls that God the Father does not desire the death of sinners, but that they return and live, alluding to Ezekiel 18:23, 32; and 33:11, 18. He also declares that God the Father loved first (1 John 4:19) and sent his Son into the world for its salvation (John 3:16). Then the priest proclaims that the Son, Jesus Christ, was handed over for the justification of sinners (Rom 4:25) and gave the Holy Spirit to his apostles for the forgiveness of sin (John 20:22-23). Finally, the priest prays that the Holy Spirit, in whom the faithful have access to the Father (Eph 2:18), may purify their hearts so that they may proclaim the deeds of the one who called them from darkness into light (1 Pet 2:9). As one draft requested,[13] the people respond, "Amen," to each part, paralleling a model from the solemn blessings in the Order of Mass.

This trinitarian content seems to be based on a longer prayer from a draft. There, to impart general absolution, the priest addressed each Person of the Trinity and concluded with a unique formula of absolution: "Send forth now, Lord, upon these your penitent servants, your Holy Spirit, who is

12. Schemata n. 297, p. 11; Schemata n. 386, p. 31.
13. Schemata n. 387 addendum II, p. 5.

the forgiveness of all sins, and by his action in them, absolve them from all sins, so that, having died with Christ, rising, they may walk with Christ in newness of life."[14]

After the threefold introduction (OP 62), the priest imparts not the usual formula of absolution, but only its key words, absolving the penitents from their sins in the name of the Father, the Son, and the Holy Spirit. Imperceptible in English except by context, the formula "I absolve you" is in the plural, as the drafts had requested.[15]

Alternatively, the priest may administer absolution in the usual form (OP 62). The words in English are the same, but the meaning of the words "you" and "your" shifts to the plural.

The ceremony concludes with some proclamation of praise or a hymn. The priest blesses and dismisses the people (OP 63).

Afterward, if the urgency relents, the forgiven penitents are to confess grave sins in person to a priest as soon as possible. This admonition appeared in the homily even in the drafts.[16] The Church requires the penitent to go to confession in this case, but it does not explicitly require the priest to give absolution on that occasion, probably because it has already taken place.

The introduction to The Order of Penance enumerates the conditions for general confession and absolution. Outside of a true emergency, the diocesan bishop is to judge the existence of these criteria. The faithful in grave sin must intend to confess the sin individually to a priest if and when the conditions for general absolution pass. They then must follow up on this intention and confess grave sins individually to a priest as soon as they have the opportunity (OP 31–34).

14. Schemata n. 386, p. 32.
15. Schemata n. 265, p. 7.
16. Schemata n. 279 bis, p. 8.

Penitential Celebrations

Background

On some occasions the faithful gather in a spirit of repentance to express their contrition and to plead for God's mercy. As outlined, these celebrations do not include the sacrament of penance, though they may help prepare for its celebration at a later date (OP Appendix II:1).

The title page of this section includes an unusual declaration, that the Vatican's Sacred Congregation for Divine Worship prepared these services to help those who organize or lead penitential celebrations. This accounts for the lack of historical antecedents for these rites, while supplying the authority for providing an aid to those who prepare and lead them.

The texts and formats are flexible (Appendix II:2–3). A local community is permitted and expected to adapt them to circumstances.

Although these outlines do not include the sacrament, those preparing the service may adjust them so that they do. In this case, after the readings and homily of the pertinent penitential celebration, the participants follow the relevant sections of the order for reconciling groups of penitents, beginning with the communal expression of sin and continuing with confession, absolution, and the concluding rites (OP Appendix II:4, citing especially OP 54–59). This section therefore provides a resource for those who are preparing a celebration of the Order for Reconciling Several Penitents with Individual Confession and Absolution.

This section presents a number of sample penitential services, arranged by theme. These begin with Lent, even before treating Advent, because Lent is the preeminent time for doing penance. The Order of Penance allows the usage of readings and prayers from the Lectionary and the Missal (OP Appendix II:6). This is all that remains of an idea from the drafts that penitential services could take place on days such as Ash Wednesday (complete with the distribution of ashes) or the weekdays of Holy Week. Such services would help a community wishing (or needing) to gather for reconciliation instead of the Eucharist, even though it calls the Lord's Supper the most powerful sign of reconciliation and salvation.[1] The Church obviously prefers that the faithful gather for the Eucharist on days such as Ash Wednesday and the weekdays of Holy Week.

All the sample celebrations follow a similar structure, though with some variations. Each may open with a song and introduction. Readings from Sacred Scripture lead to a homily and examination of conscience. Some penitential act follows, and concluding rites send the people forth.

Penitential Celebrations during Lent

The two samples of Lent take up personal and ecclesial themes. The first concerns the strengthening or restoring of the grace of baptism. The second invites fuller participation in the paschal mystery of Christ.

---

1. Schemata n. 387 addendum I, p. 3.

First Example

A draft offered catechesis on the first sample, which pertains to strengthening or restoring baptismal grace. The published book does not include this introduction, but it still explains the composition of this celebration:

> Baptism is the first and definitive participation in the death and resurrection of Christ, according to what Saint Paul wrote, "Are you unaware that we who were baptized into Christ Jesus were baptized into his death? We were indeed buried with him through baptism into death, so that, just as Christ was raised from the dead by the glory of the Father, we too might live in newness of life" (Rom 6:3-4). Because penance is the renewal of baptismal grace, it reveals its paschal character. Through it is renewed and more fully effected our immersion into the death of Christ and our rising from the dead with him.[2]

The liturgy begins with a liturgical song and greeting. The minister introduces the ceremony, which prepares the participants for the Easter Vigil, when they will recall their baptismal grace, and for the forgiveness that leads to newness of life in Christ (OP Appendix II:8). The draft specified that this ceremony prepared the participants to renew their baptismal promises at the Easter Vigil.[3] In Lent's time of purification and enlightenment, as the elect are preparing to make their baptismal promises before their baptism at the Vigil, so the faithful adopt penitential exercises to add force to their own recommitment.

The minister invites all to pray. First they kneel or bow their heads in silence. Then they stand or raise their heads, listening as the minister speaks a prayer aloud. Although penitential celebrations at other times of year follow a similar model, only

2. Schemata n. 387 addendum I, p. 4.
3. Schemata n. 387 addendum I, p. 4.

the ones in Lent call for this change in posture. The prayer that the minister recites (OP Appendix II:9) originates from the eighth-century Gelasian Sacramentary's collection of prayers for Easter evening.[4]

The proposed readings all come from the draft (OP Appendix II:10). The themes for the homily, though, were new to the published edition (11). This leads to an examination of conscience (12).

The deacon or another minister leads the penitential act, inviting all to acknowledge their sin and to call upon the mercy of God (OP Appendix II:13). The words are based on those composed for the draft, which presented them as a prayer to God, rather than an admonition to the people.[5] The introduction alludes to 2 Corinthians 6:2, the acceptable time for divine favor, and to John 15:2, the pruning of old vines and the planting of new. It cites several verses of Psalm 51 (5, 11, and 14) and concludes with an image of the land of the living (Pss 27:13 and 116:9).

Although the introduction to The Order of Penance says that penitential services may serve locations where a priest is unavailable (37), the first example introduces the priest as the minister who sprinkles the people with holy water during this final penitential act. He also offers a prayer before the concluding song and dismissal (OP Appendix II:13). This abbreviates a longer prayer in the Gelasian Sacramentary's order for those performing public penance.[6] Because the introductory comments to this section indicate that penitential services may be adapted (3), a lay presider would logically perform these actions in the absence of a priest or deacon.

4. Schemata n. 387 addendum I, p. 4, citing the Gelasian Sacramentary n. 532.

5. Schemata n. 387 addendum I, pp. 5–6.

6. Schemata n. 387 addendum I, p. 7, citing the Gelasian Sacramentary nn. 353–59.

Second Example

After a song, the minister opens the second sample with a greeting. This service intends to help the faithful understand their mutual bond of sin and repentance, and it summons individual conversion in order to sanctify the entire community (OP Appendix II:14).

The draft offered catechesis on this sample service, as it did for the first. In both cases the published edition omitted these words of introduction. Nonetheless, they give insight into the intentions of those who composed the service:

> The time of Lent is a time in which the disciples of Christ are most powerfully associated to his passion, so that, having been made sharers in his death with him, they may accomplish the salvation of the world through him and rejoice exultant with all their brothers and sisters in the resurrection of Christ. For a disciple of Christ, as the Lord himself has done, takes up the sins of the world and carries them, in order to extinguish them. Christian penitence is also born from the knowledge that as the sin of one at the same time in some way defiles and soils all, so also the conversion of one purifies and saves all others.[7]

Perhaps the published edition omitted this introduction because it overemphasized the salvific role of the community and diminished the uniqueness of Christ as the Redeemer. Nonetheless, it strove to apply the paschal mystery to the situation of individual sin and forgiveness in the midst of the Christian community.

The ceremony continues as in the first sample: The minister invites silent and spoken prayer along with an appropriate change in body postures (OP Appendix II:15). The two suggested prayers come from the draft, which does not credit

---

7. Schemata n. 387 addendum I, p. 8.

their source.[8] The revisers may have composed them. The second alludes to 2 Corinthians 4:10.

The readings and their summaries come from the draft.[9] The themes of the homily appeared only in the published edition. An examination of conscience leads to the *Confiteor* (OP Appendix II:18–19). Someone urges the faithful to perform some act of charity for the poor, the sick, or for those deprived of justice. All then recite the Lord's Prayer. A priest offers a concluding prayer, but as indicated above, another minister could logically lead this service. Or a priest, if present, could hand the leadership to another minister, reserving this final prayer for himself.

The faithful may then participate in some act of devotion, such as adoration of the cross as on Good Friday, or the Stations of the Cross as practiced in many parish churches on the Fridays of Lent. All may sing a concluding song. A greeting or blessing dismisses the people.

Penitential Celebrations during Advent

Following a similar model, a penitential celebration in Advent opens with a song and greeting (OP Appendix II:20). The presiding minister explains the purpose of the gathering, relying on Luke 12:37 in the first option and Romans 13:11-12 in the second. Both of these greetings come from the draft.[10]

The minister invites all to pray in silence (OP Appendix II:21). The two alternative prayers come from the draft, which cites the Rotulus of Ravenna as their source.[11] Dating to the seventh century or earlier, this scroll includes some of the oldest

---

8. Schemata n. 387 addendum I, p. 8.

9. Schemata n. 387 addendum I, p. 9.

10. Schemata n. 387 addendum I, p. 10.

11. Schemata n. 387 addendum I, p. 10, citing the Rotulus of Ravenna, n. 1340.

Advent prayers preserved in Christianity. (Another prayer from the same collection appears in the Missal as the collect for the Third Sunday of Advent.) The second of these prayers in The Order of Penance refers to Psalm 72:11 and Hebrews 4:15.

The proposed readings and their brief commentary come from the draft.[12] These lead to an examination of conscience. All take part in a penitential act, such as the *Confiteor*, and recite the Lord's Prayer (OP Appendix II:22–24).

The presider offers a prayer (24). Although the examples of penitential services in Lent say that a priest recites the final prayer, this one does not specify the rank of the minister. The two sample prayers come from the draft, which drew them again from the ancient Advent prayers in the Rotulus of Ravenna.[13] All may sing a fitting hymn. A minister dismisses them with a greeting or blessing.

Common Penitential Celebrations

Three celebrations adopting various themes are called "common," like the description of some prefaces in the Missal that may be used when no other preface takes precedence. These may be celebrated at any time of year, but most likely in Ordinary Time.

First Example

The first sample concerns the broad theme of sin and conversion. It opens with a hymn, such as selected verses from Psalm 139, as recommended in the draft.[14] The minister greets the people and explains the upcoming readings. The minister invites all to pray in silence and then gives voice to a prayer.

12. Schemata n. 387 addendum I, p. 11.

13. Schemata n. 387 addendum I, pp. 11–12, citing the Rotulus of Ravenna nn. 1363 and 1364.

14. Schemata n. 387 addendum I, p. 13.

This prayer considers the example of Peter's sin and tearful conversion (OP Appendix II:25), similar to the one that concludes the celebration (30). The draft used both these prayers, but in the opposite locations.[15] The new order better demonstrates the path of repentance, forgiveness, and resolve.

The proposed readings (OP Appendix II:26), all from the gospels and from the draft,[16] take an unusual structure. Luke's account of Peter's denial is told in two passages separated by silence and followed by a liturgical song, such as verses from Psalm 31 or 51. John's account of Jesus' final conversation with Simon concludes the readings. In all of Catholic worship this may be the only Liturgy of the Word featuring three gospel passages. (The same could happen in a celebration of the Rites of Immediate Preparation in the Order of Christian Initiation of Adults 185–205.)

The recommended themes for the homily (OP Appendix II:27) all come from the draft.[17] They contrast human weakness with divine mercy.

The published edition inserts an examination of conscience (OP Appendix II:28), which the draft did not so explicitly include. This fills out a sequence of elements found in the other sample penitential services. It leads to the penitential act (OP Appendix II:29), a litany of repentance taken from the draft,[18] complete with its suggestion that a different person read each intention, allowing for silent reflection each time. The introduction about God's love for humanity alludes to Romans 5:8 and 1 John 4:10. The people's response comes from Peter's declaration of the Lord's complete knowledge (John 21:17). The Lord's Prayer concludes this section.

15. Schemata n. 387 addendum I, pp. 13–14.
16. Schemata n. 387 addendum I, p. 14.
17. Schemata n. 387 addendum I, p. 14.
18. Schemata n. 387 addendum I, pp. 13–14.

The draft allowed the option for celebrating the sacrament of reconciliation at this point. The published edition removed those words. However, the introductory material permits the community to move into the elements of the Order of Reconciling Several Penitents earlier, after the homily (OP Appendix II:4).

The presiding minister, who apparently may be a member of the laity or of the clergy, offers a concluding prayer and dismisses the people (OP Appendix II:30). This is the prayer about Peter that the draft had placed near the beginning of the same celebration.

Second Example

The second common penitential celebration centers on the parable of the prodigal son who returns to his father (OP Appendix II:31–36). The entire Liturgy of the Word comes from the draft.[19] The introduction alludes to Joel 2:12, the call to return to God with all one's heart; Psalm 86:5, about God's mercy to all who call upon him; and Psalm 51:14, about receiving the joy of salvation.

The published edition expanded the homily themes with one placed at the beginning of the list: the nature of sin as a turning away from the Father's love. As in the other examples, the published edition added an examination of conscience that the draft had not included. The draft added the option of including sacramental confession,[20] which the published edition removed, as in the first example. This keeps the focus of the liturgy on non-sacramental worship.

The introduction to the penitential act declares the Lord's rich mercy, alluding to Exodus 34:6-7, and paternal welcome of the repentant sinner, as in the parable of the prodigal son

---

19. Schemata n. 387 addendum I, pp. 15–16.
20. Schemata n. 387 addendum I, p. 16.

(Luke 15:20). Even the people's response is based on the son's rehearsed words confessing his sin to his father (Luke 15:19).

The concluding prayer implies a comparison between the prodigal son and those adopted as children of God in baptism (Eph 1:5). It anticipates eternal rejoicing in God's house, as in Psalm 23:6.

Third Example

The third common penitential celebration turns to the Beatitudes for its theme (OP Appendix II:37–43). The entire liturgy comes from the draft with only a few changes.[21] It opens with an invitation to walk in newness of life (Rom 6:4).

The published edition added a theme to the homily that it placed first in the list: sin constitutes actions contrary to the Beatitudes. The draft had suggested among the homily themes the treatment of each Beatitude, but especially the hunger and thirst for justice.[22] The published edition realigned the themes to encourage imitating Christ in one's personal life, throughout the Christian community, and within human society. It then advocates a meditation on each Beatitude, without spotlighting the fourth.

The Order of Penance added an examination of conscience and removed the reference to the optional celebration of sacramental penance, as it did for the other samples of celebrations in this section. The penitential act opens with an admonition to follow in the footsteps of Christ, alluding to 1 Peter 2:21.

With minor variations, the penitential litany, based on the Beatitudes (Matt 5:3-10), comes from the draft, where the allusions to verses 4 and 5 are also in the reverse order.[23] Each petition uses the Lamb of God from the Order of Mass (130), which alludes to John 1:29, to cue and obtain the people's response.

---

21. Schemata n. 387 addendum I, pp. 17–19.
22. Schemata n. 387 addendum I, p. 17.
23. Schemata n. 387 addendum I, pp. 17–18.

For Children

In keeping with the outline from the draft,[24] the next penitential celebration is for use with children (OP Appendix II:43–53). It befits children who have not yet celebrated their first confession, and it chooses as its theme a compassionate God, who comes looking for his children. It recommends involving children in the preparation, so that they know what to say and do during the celebration (44).

As with the rest of the book, the revisers prepared the draft in Latin. The Sacred Congregation for Divine Worship published the entire typical edition, including this section, in Latin, as was its custom. The Vatican also published eucharistic prayers for Masses with children, and that typical edition is also, as expected, in Latin. However, the introduction to that collection of prayers explains that they may only be used in vernacular translation (11) because children do not speak Latin, a language that would thwart the purpose of the composition of those prayers.[25] Although The Order of Penance fails to make the same point for this celebration, logically, the principle applies here as well. It is intended for use only with vernacular translations.

The ceremony opens with another allusion to the rubric that begins the Order of Mass. As Mass begins when the people have gathered, so this penitential celebration begins when the children have gathered (OP Appendix II:45). The draft encouraged the participation of the children in various ways and the preparation of materials they may need, such as books, orders of service, and candles.[26]

The celebrant, who need not be a priest, greets the children with friendly words. Then the opening hymn takes place. This

24. Schemata n. 387 addendum I, pp. 20–23.
25. *Eucharistic Prayers for Masses with Children: For Use with the Roman Missal*, Third Edition (Washington, DC: USCCB, 2011).
26. Schemata n. 387 addendum I, p. 20.

reverses the sequence in the Order of Mass where the celebrant delays his introduction until after the opening song, sign of the cross, and greeting.

The celebrant introduces the readings before their proclamation (OP Appendix II:46). This introduction, which offers a catechesis on sin, was composed for the draft.[27] Only one reading is proclaimed (47), a gospel passage (Luke 15:1-7). Although the draft permitted proclaiming a paraphrase,[28] the published edition does not.

A rubric stresses the brevity of the homily (OP Appendix II:48), which leads to the examination of conscience (49). The published edition specifies where to find one in its appendix.

The penitential act introduces a litany of repentance for sins common among children (OP Appendix II:50). The published edition lightly edited the words from the draft.[29] The Lord's Prayer concludes the litany.

Individual children may then come forward, light a candle, and declare a particular resolution for doing good (OP Appendix II:51). Alternatively, they may set a written intention on a table or recite a general intention together. All these suggestions came from the draft.[30]

The celebrant offers a prayer (OP Appendix II:52). A minister, who may be someone other than the celebrant, invites the children to give thanks, possibly in a song (53). The same minister then dismisses the children. The draft envisioned that the celebrant blessed the children before dismissing them.[31] However, probably because a layperson may preside over the entire ceremony, the published edition omits such a blessing.

27. Schemata n. 387 addendum I, p. 21.
28. Schemata n. 387 addendum I, p. 21.
29. Schemata n. 387, p. 22.
30. Schemata n. 387, p. 22.
31. Schemata n. 387, p. 23.

For Young People

The introductory note to this ceremony promotes the inclusion of youth in the preparation and execution of the liturgy. They may help select the texts and songs. They may exercise many of the ministries (OP Appendix II:54). The draft explained the reason for this: that the young people truly make this their own celebration.[32]

Its theme is the renewal of one's life according to the Christian vocation. The draft expressed the theme less articulately: the renewal of vocation and of the Christian life.[33]

The greeting sets a positive tone, detailing the fruits of conversion rather than the difficulties of repentance (OP Appendix II:55). It alludes to Philippians 3:13, where Paul urges forgetting the past and straining for the future; Romans 8:21, about the freedom of the children of God; and Matthew 13:46, about the pearl of great price. The speaker is not defined. Logically, it would be the presider, but in theory any of the youth could deliver this introduction, in keeping with the advice from the opening rubric.

All sing about God's call to new life and the Christian's pursuit of it. The words of Psalm 40:1-9 are recommended, along with a refrain expressing one's desire to do God's will.

The prayer addresses God as the one who calls the faithful from darkness into light, as in 1 Peter 2:9 (OP Appendix II:56). Again, the rubric assigns this prayer to no particular minister. Typically, a presider reads such a part, but it could be shared by another representative of the youth.

For the readings, the draft recommended "Galatians 5:1. 13f, 2."[34] It is hard to interpret what that means; perhaps verses 1 and 13-26 of chapter 5. The draft's reference to chapter 5 verse 2 (or all of chapter 2?) makes no sense. Perhaps that

32. Schemata n. 387 addendum I, p. 24.
33. Schemata n. 387 addendum I, p. 24.
34. Schemata n. 387 addendum I, p. 25.

is why the published edition changed this to a choice between Romans 7:18-25 and Romans 8:19-23. As in the draft, the published edition calls for song or silence after this reading, to be followed by Matthew 13:44-46 (OP Appendix II:57).

For the homily, the themes resemble those of other penitential celebrations. However, as in the case of the second and third examples of the common celebrations and the one for children, the published edition added a theme to the top of the list: confronting sin, which makes us struggle against God (OP Appendix II:58). The homily leads to an examination of conscience.

The draft offered an alternative integration of reading, exhortation, and examination, led by three readers respectively. The published edition did not include it. However, in the interests of studying the development of these penitential services, and given the flexibility allowed in their celebration, its content and unique structure merit attention:

> Reading—Exhortation—Examination of Conscience
>
> Reader 1: It is God who opens the meaning and purpose of our life for us. Therefore, let us hear the Word of God that in its light we may judge our habits, actions and character of our life. The prophet Ezekiel speaks in the name of God: (Ezek 36:25-27).
>
> Reader 2: God pours his Holy Spirit into our hearts. It is he who gives us life that is not simply ours but God's. Strengthened by his power, we can overcome egoism and all the things that block service of God and our brothers and sisters. He makes us saints and living members of the holy Church of God. Therefore, this is our vocation: that we may bear witness to the life-giving Spirit of God, and to the goodness of God, who leads us from the weakness of a life surrendered to vanity and makes us companions of his divine nature.
>
> Reader 3: Therefore, let each of us question ourselves by examining our conscience: Am I truly happy about

my vocation to the Christian life? Do I thank God for the gift of the Holy Spirit, who teaches me to understand the mysteries of the reign of God and who is at work in me for the good? Am I prompt and diligent upon hearing the voice of God, who speaks to me in the Church of his Son and in my conscience? Do I tend to prayer (daily) and participate actively in the celebration of Mass and of the other divine offices (at least on Sundays and feast days)?

(Time of silence.)

Reader 1: Deservedly, great people create freedom. Many, however, do not know what true freedom is, where it comes from, and to what purpose it has been given to us. The apostle Paul writes in the Letter to the Galatians: (Gal 5:1, 13-26).[35]

Reader 2: Christ our Lord has called us to true freedom. He, the powerful one, suffered for us on the cross in the greatest freedom, in order to free us from slavery to sin. Our freedom has been purchased at such a great price! It is now up to us to understand it and to guide it toward the purpose that Christ willed. For only a person set free from the power of evil through Christ can be lord of oneself and form together with others a world according to the will of God.

Reader 3: Therefore, let us each ask ourselves: What passions hold me in servitude? Do I indulge my desires? Am I prepared to take control of my evil inclinations? Do I regularly apply myself to the development of my gifts and talents? Do I follow only my will, or do I attend to the freedom of others and respect their rights? Am I truthful, faithful, diligent? Am I ready to work together in the Church and in society so that, united in strength, we may form a world full of justice and peace according to the will of God?

(Time of silence).

---

35. Literally, "Gal 5, 1.13f," but these verses are the most logical.

Reader 1: Our habits can easily keep our conscience from hearing the true gift that God gives us by calling us into his reign. Because we are inattentive, we therefore imagine with difficulty the human situation, the meaning and purpose of a person's life, and that from childhood we have lived in the light of divine revelation. Therefore we do not often notice how much our life and the lives of others suffer damnation if we prefer other goods to the reign of God. Let us hear what Jesus says about the inestimable value of the reign of God, while showing us how to enter it (Matt 13:44-46).

Reader 2: Christ himself, the true witness, teaches us that the reign of God is the highest good to which no other good can be compared. In baptism we have been called members of this reign. In confirmation we received the fullness of the Spirit, with whose power the reign of God is built and expands throughout the world by means of the Church of Christ. The true development of our life and the perfection of the world depend on it, whether or not we understand the treasure of our vocation with all our strength.

Reader 3: Let us each now ask ourselves whether our life corresponds to so great a vocation: Do I value honor, possessions and other similar things more than my Christian vocation? Do I freely profess Christianity among my peers, colleagues and relatives, in private and public life? Do I cultivate a better and growing knowledge of my faith as best as I am able? Am I conscious of the obligation to advance by word and example an increase of the reign of God? Am I ready to work with the religious and social activities of the Church?

(If it was not already done before in the places indicated, a notable time of silence is made.)[36]

In the published service, after the examination of conscience, the penitential act follows as someone invites all to

36. Schemata n. 387 addendum I, pp. 25–27.

recite the *Confiteor*. The invitation alludes to Christ's call of sinners in Matthew 9:13; Mark 2:17; and Luke 5:32. A minister leads a litany and then invites all to offer the Lord's Prayer. All may sing a song before they are dismissed (OP Appendix II:60–61).

For the Sick

The Order of Penance also proposes a model penitential service for the sick. Its theme, "The Time of Sickness is a Time of Grace," eschews the false theological assumption that all sickness results from sin. Instead, it helps the sick encounter the grace of God at a time they feel especially in need. The ritual does not indicate the venue for this celebration, but one could easily imagine it taking place inside a public building that specializes in care for the sick.

The order of service (OP Appendix II:62–73) is based on one from the draft.[37] The presiding minister greets the people, reminding them that Jesus framed his message of repentance as good news (Mark 1:15), and encouraging the mutual forgiveness of trespasses (Matt 6:12). The sick may sing a hymn, or a choir may sing on their behalf (OP Appendix II:63). The minister offers a prayer that the revisers apparently composed for this occasion (64).

An introduction to the readings is supplied without indicating who delivers it. The draft assigned it to either the reader or the celebrant.[38] It alludes to Colossians 1:24, the encouraging passage that joins human suffering to the sufferings of Christ.

The readings are classic biblical passages pertaining to illness. They tell of presbyters of the apostolic church anointing the sick (Jas 5:13-16) and of Jesus healing the sick while forgiving sin (Mark 2:1-12). Psalm 51 or 130 may be recited or sung in alternation between the readings (OP Appendix II:66).

37. Schemata n. 387 addendum I, pp. 29–32.
38. Schemata n. 387 addendum I, p. 29.

The homily is to focus on the failings of the soul, rather than on the weakness of the body, and on the power of the Church to forgive sins and the power of suffering offered for others (OP Appendix II:67). The draft proposed one additional theme: the communitarian nature not only of sin but also of care for the sinner.[39] Its omission perhaps keeps the focus on the sick, rather than on their caregivers, who have other opportunities for penitential celebrations.

For the examination of conscience, the usual appendix provides help. The ritual supplies additional questions pertaining to the conditions of the sick, their temptations to despair, the use of their time, and their appreciation of caregivers. One again alludes to Colossians 1:24, which sees sickness as an opportunity to suffer with Christ (OP Appendix II:68).

The penitential act opens with the *Confiteor* and leads to a litany that expresses remorse to each Person of the Holy Trinity. The minister invites all to recite the Lord's Prayer (OP Appendix II:69).

A choir or the assembly may sing a hymn. This leads to a brief litany of thanksgiving, alluding to 2 Corinthians 1:3, by calling upon the God of consolation, the Father of mercies. The second element again refers to Colossians 1:24 (OP Appendix II:70–71).

The concluding prayer may be replaced with a blessing, an option that presumes that the minister leading the ceremony is a deacon or priest. In place of the usual dismissal, the minister may invite visitors who participated in the celebration to stay for a while and converse with the sick (OP Appendix II:72–73).

39. Schemata n. 387 addendum I, p. 30.

Examination of Conscience

The last appendix of The Order of Penance presents a form for the examination of one's conscience (OP Appendix III:1–3). After some general introductory questions, it offers additional ones based on three passages from the gospels: Matthew 22:37 about loving God with all one's heart, John 15:12 about loving one another, and John 14:21 about keeping the commandments of Christ.

The draft presented nine different formulas for this examination, stretching over fifteen pages, all carried out within a liturgical service. They involve a leader, a reader, and the assembly responding to various litanies and prayers. The published edition abandoned this format in favor of a series of questions helping an individual's examination of conscience before coming to participate in the sacrament of penance.

A translation of all nine of these formulas is provided here as an insight into the history of twentieth-century liturgy and an extra tool for those preparing examinations of conscience.

I.

Priest (Reader): We confess that, led by prejudices, we have inconsiderately and unjustly judged and not wanted to understand or respect others.

We confess that we have only turned toward those who are important to us or who have joined up with us, and we have avoided those who are bothersome or burdensome to us.

We have committed offenses because we have restricted our conscience from unpleasant matters of reality and chosen pretense.

We are weak because we trust more in our deliberations and thoughts than in the Word of God, which we hear freely if it seems to respond to our opinions, but not if it makes a judgment about us.

Father, we have sinned, but putting trust in Jesus Christ, we dare to say, as he taught us to pray:

All: Our Father . . .

II.

Priest (or Reader): We each confess on our own, but also as the family of Jesus Christ, that we have sinned and committed offenses, that we were slow in fulfilling the demands of faith, in exercising each responsibility, in work or in study, in sustaining various relationships among other people, in showing faithfulness to God.

We confess our failure.

(Silence.)

All: Lamb of God, who take away the sin of the world, have mercy on us.

Priest (Reader): God desires to be sought, but we are dulled and hardened. We hinder ourselves and often flee into worry, into skepticism, into sloth. We have been deprived of God also by our offense and negligence.

(Silence.)

All: Lamb of God, who take away the sin of the world, have mercy on us.

Priest (or Reader): As Christians we have concealed the gospel by the way we live. Wherever we spend our time, we share offenses regarding the misery by which people afflict themselves; we impose burdens on others. If only we had been disturbed by this!

(Silence.)

All: Lamb of God, who take away the sin of the world, have mercy on us.

Priest (or Reader): Contending with others, we often seek ourselves and use others as if they were only the stage upon which we ourselves appear. In relations with others we are often found false and negligent, we reject others or we avoid those who seek us.

(Silence.)

All: Lamb of God, who take away the sin of the world, have mercy on us.

(After a time of silence, all say):

I confess . . .

(And/or):

Our Father . . .

Priest: O Lord, our God, forgive our sins. Your command, according to which we ought to forgive the sins of others, leads us into tribulations. For often with an angry spirit we insist on our own will. How will we ever be able to come to your Son, Jesus Christ? We ask that you direct us toward him. For he is our grace, the forgiveness of sins, and the one greater than any thinkable offense. He is law and justice for us, for this world, for all time.

All: Amen.

III.

Priest: Paul the apostle says: Through Christ, God gave the ministry of reconciliation to us (2 Cor 5:18). On behalf of Christ we act as priests by delegation. God appeals through us. We implore on behalf of Christ, "Be reconciled to God" (5:20). Let us therefore be prepared for reconciliation, seeking pardon of one another now in church before God.

I myself seek pardon from you and from all whom I have failed as a priest and shepherd of souls, but also as a neighbor.
(Silence.)
Priest: Let married couples here and at home seek pardon for wounded love, every impatience, and an ungrateful spirit.
(Silence.)
Priest: Let adolescents seek pardon because they have encouraged one another to sin and wrongly squandered their desires and trust.
(Silence.)
Priest: Let employers seek pardon from their coworkers and employees, and these also from their employers, for carrying out unjust treatment, harm, the demand of too much work, and committing bad performance at work.
(Silence.)
Priest: Let parents seek pardon from children, for every imprudent order, undue soft-heartedness, meagerness of time reserved for them, and applying truly excessive severity. And let children seek pardon of their parents for disobedience, and for lack of love and gratitude.
(Silence.)
Priest: Let each one who has hatred for others pursue reconciliation, for the gospel says, "If you forgive others their transgressions, your heavenly Father will forgive you" (Matt 6:14).
(Silence.)
All of us who have often hurt the reputation of another ought to restore it; and we ought to repair the damage we inflicted on others.
(Silence.)
Priest: In this way, reconciliation has entered our community, and conversion and repentance have come to each person. This is the will of God, that we all be converted with our whole heart.

He will help us in this hour, so that each may come to meet the other, and that all of us thus come together to him. Let us now pray together, as Christ himself taught us: Our Father . . .

IV.

Reader I: God asks us that the desire for communicating with others shape our whole life. The apostle Paul wrote to the Galatians, "Bear one another's burdens, and so you will fulfill the law of Christ" (6:2).

Reader II: Do I refuse to take care of others, or do I engage with them? Was I attentive to others, skillful at being considerate toward them, that I might know what they expect of me, carefully giving them the better part, which they desired, and speaking with them in a friendly way, which they also wanted? Was I looking out on their behalf for what was able to help them? How much thought have I given this? Did I present myself generous and cordial toward those with whom I live? (Silence.)

Reader I: God asks us to share our external possessions. Paul wrote to the Corinthians, "Consider this: whoever sows sparingly will also reap sparingly, and whoever sows bountifully will also reap bountifully. Each must do as already determined, without sadness or compulsion, for God loves a cheerful giver" (2 Cor 9:6-7).

Reader II: Was I perhaps able to give from my possessions, even if I would have to live more sparingly? Was I able to spend more time with others? Was I happy to receive a brother or sister coming to me, whose need was perhaps a sight not so welcome for me? Did I do my part in the family, which ought to be "a school of sharing rightly," to lift up others in the necessities of life? (Silence.)

Reader I: God also asks of us that we be ready to share in spiritual matters. Again Paul wrote to the Corinthians: "I urge you, brothers [and sisters], in the name of our Lord Jesus Christ, that all of you agree in what you say, and that there be no divisions among you, but that you be united in the same mind and in the same purpose" (1 Cor 1:10).

Reader II: Did I try to understand the mind of others and listen to it? Did I rejoice with those who rejoice or envy them? Did I show compassion for the sorrows of others? Did I truly keep the promise of praying for another? We have been blessed in having faith; but did I do anything to share this faith with others and communicate it with them? Was I able also to speak in the family about matters that are deeper than those that surround us? Was I able to communicate religious life together with others and pray with them?

(Silence.)

Reader I: God asks also that we all remain joined in the care of the Church, and that all be concerned about all the churches. Again Paul says, "And apart from these things, there is the daily pressure upon me of my anxiety for all the churches. Who is weak, and I am not weak? Who is led to sin, and I am not indignant?" (2 Cor 11:28-29).

Reader II: Did I do work for the Church and the world beyond my private concerns? Was I convinced that the concern for the Church also applies to me together with the pope and the bishops? What did I do that the parishes and Christian communities where I live became part of my heart? What did I do to recommend this to others?

And above all: Did I pray daily for the needs of the universal Church?

What was the greatest impediment to my Christian life this year, especially this Lent? What especially separated me from God and from others?

V.

Reader I: Let us undergo an examination whether or not we put the demands of life into practice.

First let us ask what we did in relation to ourselves.

It is inexcusable if anyone
—content with mediocrity, once and for all, does not attempt to forsake it;
—does not find time for silence, meditation, reflection;
—customarily acts badly;
—firmly goes without offering and following advice.
(Silence.)
Reader I: Lord, we have sinned.
All: Have mercy and forgive us our trespasses.
Reader II: Let us ask what we did in relation to others.

It is inexcusable if anyone
—does not help another because of laziness;
—only spends time with those whose friendship can bear fruit;
—remains silent out of fear, shyness, or pride, when they ought to profess the truth;
—conceals from their spouse the use of their profits and revenue;
—commits to some matter outside the home in their free time without speaking beforehand with their spouse;
—so performs the conjugal act that it does not become an expression of ever-growing love;
—loves common prayer in the family only a little bit, and performs it mechanically and never participates in the liturgy together with the whole family.
(Silence.)
Reader II: Lord, we have sinned.
All: Have mercy and forgive us our trespasses.
Reader I: Let parents examine their life!

It is inexcusable if anyone
—scarcely or not even scarcely wants to become more certain about questions of education or to accept advice;
—thinks it is enough that children be as educated as they themselves were once educated;
—leaves education to the mother alone;
—completely prohibits the conception of children;
—treats adolescents like infants.
Reader II: Let adolescents examine their life!

It is inexcusable if anyone

—thinks that the problems of the world do not pertain to oneself and concerns oneself only with the newest sport and music;

—treats parents like slaves;

—argues every fact, conversation, and opinion of parents and teachers, leading them to speak about the way things used to be and with excessive authority;

—falls in love with an adolescent of the opposite sex, thinking nothing about responsibility and considering love as some kind of game;

—never seeks to grow internally through friendship with a girl, but considers her as a mere amusement;

—completely ignores institutions, especially religion. (Silence.)

Reader I: We have sinned.

We speak freely about charity, of bringing help, of ministry toward others, but we flee opportunities. We abhor inhumanity and oppression, but we do not care about the needs of a neighbor: the foreign workers in our city, those who struggle with drug addiction, drunks, mothers with infants born of unknown fathers. We ask for justice in the country and society, but we are not ready to act in public. Nor have we even tried to love our enemies and adversaries. We avoid, do not understand, and disregard them. We have deceived others by lying, we have belittled their honor; thus we have attacked them as with whips, though we have not been struck. We have not been crucified as was Christ, but we have crucified others, and we have crucified them for what we thought was wrong. We spend money recklessly, while at the same time countless people are thirsty and go about hungry.

Lord, we have sinned.

All: Have mercy and forgive us our trespasses.

Reader II: Lord, we are bound by obligations.

We all know that; each one knows that.

Yet we cannot list what our obligations are.

If we announce our sins, the act is often worthy of ridicule.

Let us focus just on children and know already that
we owe much to them.

Let us consider our spouse and, without pretense, let
us be aware of our sins of denying love: our egoism, the
vice of finding fault with all things, and our rights that
we never want to waive.

And if we remember our neighbor, the sick, those
needing help, and the poor of every kind, Lord, then we
no longer have to look for our sins, for then our fault
oppresses us. Doesn't the same thing happen to us before
you? Should we not contemplate you to grasp how much
we stand apart from you?

Speak to us in this celebration that we may contemplate you, see you, and stand before you.

We can perceive you so that we not lose hope.

We can be conscious of guilt before you lest it crush
us.

If we carry our sins around with us, they oppress us
and make us blind.

If we confess them to you, we are set free and we see.

O Lord, overcome whatever separates us from you.

Cover up the ditch that we always dig between you
and us.

Lord, have mercy on us!

Priest: Before we all pronounce our confession together,
each one ought to clearly answer wherever they did not
respond to the questions in relation to themselves, to
others, and to God, and wherever they may have personal guilt.

(Silence.)

All: I confess to almighty God . . .

VI.

Priest: The Pharisees wanted to interrogate Jesus. Jesus,
though, gave a response that reduced them to silence,
indeed that interrogated them. In this state of affairs, one
confession must be made: "Lord, I have loved little."

Reader: Let us be interrogated by the Word of God.

Whom do we love?

Do we truly love others or do we think only of ourselves?

Do we love only those who also love us?

Do we disregard the misery that we see?

Let us think about the day just passed, about the last weeks or months of our life in light of the request that we ought to love our neighbors as ourselves.

What does God mean for us?

Is God a mere governance of the administration of the world, whose laws must be kept, or is he the Father of our Lord Jesus Christ, the God who so loved us that he gave his only Son for us?

Are we moved by this love of God?

Do we know that God desires us and not only our good behavior?

Let us think about what God means for us.

(Silence.)

Reader: Father, we have sinned against you.

All: Father, we have sinned against you.

Reader: We have committed sin against others.

All: Father, we have sinned against you.

Reader: We have committed sin against those who are neighbors to us.

All: Father, we have sinned against you.

Reader: We have committed sin against the community of your Son, against the Church.

All: Father, we have sinned against you.

Reader: We have committed sin against you.

All: Father, we have sinned against you.

Reader: Father, forgive us.

All: Father, forgive us.

Reader: We confess our guilt to one another.

All: Father, forgive us.

Reader: We confess our guilt before the Church.

All: Father, forgive us.

Reader: We confess our guilt before you.

All: Father, forgive us.

VII. Regarding Truth

Priest: Let us now investigate the way we behave and our offenses against truth.

Reader: We confess how much the absence of truth renders human communal life more difficult and dangerous: in the family, among friends, between neighbors, in the workplace, in shops, in society, and among peoples.

Therefore each of us ought to ask ourselves, Do I affirm the responsibility of presenting myself truthfully and sincerely? Have I tended to myself correctly so that I may behave?

Have I been led, although I had been provided with the truth, into lying, deception, leading others into error, calumny, and false accusation?

Have I striven to be virtuous, upright, reliable, faithful, and reserved? Have I betrayed secrets? Was I gullible or distrusting? Have I exhibited a zealous spirit or did I damage the truth out of fear of other people?

(Silence.)

All: I confess to almighty God . . .

VIII.

Priest: The world has been ensnared in the net of sin and guilt. We are all attached to that net in which we are held. For everything that we do immediately also pertains to others. Every sin harms others. Every sin is a stone in the wall we build between ourselves and God.

Reader I: Everywhere on earth dwell enmities, hatreds, lies, injustices, violence, and wars. There are people like us who hate and do not love, who disdain and do not understand, who argue and do not make peace. Each of us shares the guilt that people daily inflict upon themselves.

Reader II: We are members of humanity, but we are yet more intimately the people of God, the Church. Also in the Church dwell egoism, hardness, imprudence, inhumanity, envy, and disparagement. There are Christians like us who are not mindful of the events in the world, who do not care about the prosperity of every person, who feel that they are chosen and disdain others, and who want to rule and not serve. Each of us shares the guilt that distorts the image of Christ and the Church.

Reader III: Discord begins because we ourselves are not of one heart. We ourselves do not judge the other favorably. We do not tolerate someone else's greater success. We disparage the one who hardens our conscience. We are impatient. We ignore the truth if that helps us.

Do we care about justice, love, and peace, or do we hope for these things only from others? From the Church? From humanity?

We all bring our own guilt, but also the guilt of the Church and of the world.

Priest: O Lord, we bring the guilt of all the world before you. Often we do not want to be made conscious of this, but we confess to you today that we share the guilt for the misery of humanity. We have not used all the possibilities to hinder the guilt of others. We also bring this outside guilt before you. For it is not right that we stand apart from the guilt of others.

O Lord, we confess our sin.

All: O Lord, we confess our sin.

Priest: O Lord, we have often lived as if you and your command to love others did not exist. We often stay in the middle, not fully living as Christians. We were happy with our guilt and the guilt of others, and we did not love anew.

O Lord, we confess our sin.

All: O Lord, we confess our sin.

Priest: O Lord, sin shakes us only a bit. We do not suffer enough from it, especially if we did not commit it. We leave others alone in their guilt, and we think that we can flee evil in this way.

O Lord, we confess our sin.

All: O Lord, we confess our sin.

Reader I: The one incapable of forgiving remains hard. Such a one closes in on oneself and does not find a way toward others. Community is the responsibility of all of us. Only in it is human life fully realized and receives value. We experience sin and guilt as the permanent threat to living together. The one who always counters sin with sin obstructs new beginnings. Such people build a wall between themselves and others.

Reader II: This is the bothersome state of things in our land: Because people, rulers, and powers want to prevail, peace becomes impossible. But what matters to East and West, to peoples, nations, and regions, also matters between old and young, parents and children, among neighbors, companions, and ourselves.

Reader III: The command of God is: You are indeed brothers and sisters. Therefore let us be prepared to forgive. Let us seek to break the chains of sins and increase reconciliation.

Priest: O Lord, grant us the courage to forgive.

All: O Lord, grant us the courage to forgive.

Priest: If we argue among ourselves,

All: O Lord, grant us the courage to forgive.

Priest: If others act unjustly toward us,

All: O Lord, grant us the courage to forgive.

Priest: If we diminish the honor of others and sustain suspicions about them,

All: O Lord, grant us the courage to forgive.

Priest: In the fight of peoples, classes, and ideologies,

All: O Lord, grant us the courage to forgive.

Priest: We ought to forgive seventy times seven times every day.

All: O Lord, grant us the courage to forgive.

IX.

Priest: Let us confess our guilt before Jesus and obtain his forgiveness.

Reader: We have done evil out of wrath and hatred, out of pride and arrogance. We confess this and we ask pardon.

(Silence.)

Reader: Christ, hear us.

All: Christ, hear us.

Reader: We have avoided the good out of negligence and laziness because we have thought only about ourselves. We confess this and we ask pardon.

(Silence.)

Reader: Christ, hear us.

All: Christ, hear us.

Reader: We have not obeyed the Word of God. We have choked it in the concern for our life. We confess this and we ask pardon.

(Silence.)

Reader: Christ, hear us.

All: Christ, hear us.

Reader: We have been ungrateful toward God. We have closed ourselves off from his grace. We confess this and we ask pardon.

(Silence.)

Reader: Christ, hear us.

All: Christ, hear us.[1]

1. Schemata n. 387 addendum I, pp. 33–47.

Conclusion: Be Renewed

The sacrament of reconciliation, which concerns the renewal of the sinner, has itself undergone renewal. Throughout its history the Church has offered forgiveness in different forms: a once-in-a-lifetime opportunity for those who made commitments at baptism but then failed to keep them, an expansion of spiritual direction growing from remote monasteries through distant missions, an intense anonymous conversation between penitent and priest, a haven for serious sinners, a consolation for those annoyed by previously absolved peccadillos, and an occasion for communal confession and forgiveness.

The Catholic Church took advantage of a period of liturgical renewal in the years after the Second Vatican Council to renew this sacrament again. Its nature and effects were studied in the light of this history. The study group for the revision broadly consulted members of the Church, both experts and ordinary practitioners, and received feedback to encourage and challenge their work. Some of revisers' ideas did not advance very far, such as having one priest absolve the sins of all who confessed individually at a communal penance service. Some of their proposals never saw the light of day, such as the extensive repertoire of examinations of conscience. Still, their work shows the spirit of the times—open to renewal, committed to serious historical investigation, and devoted to pastoral sensitivity. They also boldly changed the quintuple form of absolution from the previous Roman Ritual into a simpler, more theologically expressive declaration. Yet even that took extensive discussion and careful analysis, word by word.

Through their survey of historical sources, the revisers reclaimed certain prayers and traditions. For example, the Rotulus of Ravenna, a source unknown to those who formed the seventeenth-century Roman Ritual, provided some prayers for use in the communal celebrations in Advent. The Roman Pontifical's rituals for reconciling the order of penitents provided a framework for communal celebrations, as well as a font of orations, postures, occasions, and ministers. The renewal of the sacrament after the council gave wider access to traditions of previous generations.

Putting the entire celebration into the vernacular languages of the world was itself an exercise of renewal. In its origins, the complete ritual would have used the language of the people. The conversation between the penitent and the priest would always transpire in their own languages, but important parts, such as absolution, took place in Latin. After the reforms, penitents were again able to experience the entire ceremony in their own language.

For anglophones, the first translation accomplished much good. It helped convey the nature and effects of the sacrament to all those participating in its celebration. The second English translation builds on that. Following the revised rules of translation and approval processes, it provides a more consistent feel to the words that people know, even as it introduces some precisions that the first translation left indistinct. The 2023 publication of a revised English translation is another example of how the sacrament of reconciliation has been renewed.

All of this work benefits the penitent, a sinner who has come to terms with his or her own misdeeds, expressed dissatisfaction with them, and who seeks not only personal forgiveness, but reconciliation with God and with other members of the Church. The penitent's own renewal serves as a paradigm for the application of principles of the liturgical renewal. The willingness of the Church to explore the liturgies of the past, honestly confront the opportunities for betterment, and propose new paths forward, models for each Christian the spiritual journey from past behavior to future glory. In practice, when the priest and the penitent are attentive to a meaningful celebration of The Order of Penance, the community of the Church—and each individual within it—will be renewed.